How to create a gender balance in political decision-making

A guide to implementing policies for increasing the participation of women in political decision-making

by Monique Leijenaar

in collaboration with the European experts network
'Women in decision-making'

Employment & social affairs

Equal opportunities

European Commission
Directorate-General for Employment, Industrial Relations and Social Affairs
Unit V/D.5

Manuscript finished in March 1996

Monique Leijenaar is Professor of Political Science at the University of Nijmegen, Netherlands. She specializes in local politics, election studies and women and politics and has published several articles and books on these topics. She has worked as a consultant for the Dutch government as well as intergovernmental organizations. From 1992 to 1996 she was the Dutch representative in the European experts network 'Women in decision-making'.

$\mathcal{DB} \# 1449/33$

This guide was financed by and prepared for the use of the European Commission, Directorate-General for Employment, Industrial Relations and Social Affairs. It does not necessarily represent the Commission's official position.

ZZ
EM24
97H51

A great deal of additional information on the European Union is available on the Internet. It can be accessed through the Europa server (http://europa.eu.int)

Cataloguing data can be found at the end of this publication

Luxembourg: Office for Official Publications of the European Communities, 1997

ISBN 92-827-9833-X

Printed in Italy

Table of contents

Concluding remarks   59

Notes   61

Appendices   65

Introduction

Historical background

The problem of ensuring that women are at the centre of political decision-making is now very topical in Europe. In the EU countries the average percentage of women in parliament (lower and upper house) is 15% and in cabinet 16%. However, there is considerable variation between countries in numerical representation as well as in the willingness to improve the political participation of women. In Belgium, for example, the government has introduced legislation demanding that political parties nominate 33% women on their list of candidates. In Italy comparable legislation for candidates in elections at the local level, which was introduced in 1993, was declared unconstitutional in 1995. In Luxembourg, there was, until 1996, not one single policy to address the situation. However in March 1996 the Luxembourg Parliament adopted a motion which paves the way to introducing quotas in the constitution in order to achieve a gender balance of 40-60%.

In most European countries women won the right to vote around 1920. By then the struggle for women's suffrage had taken many years, due to opposition based mainly on the conception that a woman's proper role was in the family. The advent of suffrage for women raised questions about the consequences of doubling the electorate. Since then, there has been an ongoing debate on the role of women in politics. Compared to 75 years ago, however, the general attitude towards the political integration of women is much more positive and these days there are few who hold the view that women do not belong in politics. It is even widely admitted that unbalanced representation in political decision-making embodies a deficit for democracy. The current debate thus focuses primarily on the question of *how*, not *whether*, to increase the participation of women in politics.

This positive attitude can be found also in official statements and resolutions from international agencies. Already in 1960, the International Covenant on Civil and Political Rights stated: 'The States party to the present covenant undertake to ensure the equal right of men and women to the enjoyment of all civil and political rights set forth in the present covenant'. At the European level, the Council of Ministers adopted the following resolution on 27 March 1995: 'The Council affirms that balanced participation in decision-making ... in every sphere of life constitutes an important condition for equality between men and women. It is necessary to make every effort to bring about the changes in structures and attitudes which are essential for genuine equality of access to decision-making posts for men and women in the political, economic, social and cultural fields'.

The most recent world-wide statement can be found in the Platform for Action based on the Fourth World Conference in Beijing organized by the United Nations. Governments have approved the following text: 'governments commit themselves to establishing the goal of gender balance in governmental bodies and committees, as well as in public administrative entities, and in the judiciary, including *inter alia* setting specific targets and implementing measures to substantially increase the number of women with a view to achieving equal representation of women and men' (par.190a) and 'to take measures, including, where appropriate, in electoral systems that encourage political parties to integrate women in elective and non-elective public positions in the same proportion and at the same levels as men'.

Finally, there is a Commission proposal for a Council Recommendation on the balanced participation of women and men in decision-making. It proposed that the Council of Ministers recommend that the Member States adopt an integrated strategy and develop or introduce suitable legislative or regulatory measures or incentives for achieving a gender balance in decision-making. Such a strategy should cover all spheres of society in partnership with all social actors involved at European national, regional and local levels.

Objective and contents of this guide

This guide is meant to assist governments, political parties and NGOs of the EU countries in putting into action their positive attitude to the empowerment of women into concrete, integrated policies leading to an increase in the number of women in political positions. In many countries governments have undertaken activities, as is described in the next chapters, but in most countries these are *ad hoc* activities and not part of an integrated overall policy aimed at increasing women's political participation. In this guide we present a blueprint for a national policy plan which, with a few adaptations, governments can use to develop such an overall policy on the participation of women in political decision-making. Besides governments, this guide can be helpful to political parties and women's organizations in their efforts to increase the political participation of women.

The guide consists of two parts. In the first part, in Chapters 1 and 2, we sketch the context for a national policy plan. We start in **Chapter 1** with an analysis of the problem: an outline of the present numerical situation in EU countries and arguments in favour of women's participation in political decision-making. This is followed in **Chapter 2** by an overview of explanations of women's under-representation in politics. The distinction between individual and institutional characteristics is used to categorize the different barriers for women trying to enter the political arena. Based on the numerous studies of the under-represen-tation of women, especially in legislative bodies, it is possible to present an aggregate overview of the factors which may help women to enter high level political decision making. These include the social and political climate of a country, gender equality, the electoral system and the selection processes and selection criteria used in political parties. We conclude Part 1 by arguing that increasing the number of women in political decision-making is also a way to solve the current crisis of (party) politics that concerns all Member States.

The second part describe the tools. The main part of a national policy plan is a list of concrete activities and plans that the government should undertake in order to reach a gender balance in political decision-making. Since the choice for specific measures is country-specific, we present in **Chapter 3** many different instruments a government can introduce. To stress the practicality of this guide we discuss the pros and cons of these policies and give many examples of countries where these instruments have actually been introduced. Although governments are the primary movers in empowering women, political parties also play an important role. This is because in most countries political parties not only select the political personnel for cabinet and parliament, but often also make the selections for elective positions at regional and local level. As is the case with governmental activities we find in some countries that political parties have an overall programme to mobilize women within its ranks, while in other countries political parties have not been very active in this regard. Because of the pivotal role of parties, some of the instruments that are described in **Chapter 4** are directed at them.

In **Chapter 4** a blueprint of a national policy plan will be presented. With a few adaptations by national governments, this plan can be used in every EU country. Three examples of relevant policy programmes are presented here: plans made by the Belgium Government, by the Netherlands Government and by the Swedish Government. The last part in this chapter consists of presenting activities promoted by the European Commission in this field.

The guide concludes with the argument that engaging more women in political leadership can also be helpful in restoring some of the belief in politics and democracy.

Part I — Background

Chapter 1
The importance of a gender balance: defining the problem

Europe has more than 370 million inhabitants and 51% of them are women. Despite the fact that equality between men and women is one of the founding principles of European Community legislation, women remain significantly under-represented in political decision-making both on a European level and in the representative bodies of the Member States.

In this chapter we present some recent figures about the participation of women in representative bodies, followed by several arguments about why more women should participate in political decision-making.

1.1. Figures on women in political decision-making

Women's participation in political decision-making began with the arrival of universal suffrage. In 10 of the 15 EU countries the right of women to vote was granted at the beginning of this century and often after extended struggles. The opposition against the enfranchisement of women was based mainly on the conception that women did not belong in politics: women were too emotional and therefore not capable of evaluating political matters; women were already represented through their husbands and interfering with such a 'dirty' matter as politics would lead to a loss of femininity.[1] Through parades, demonstrations, sit-ins, hunger strikes and marches on the parliament, women demanded equal political rights and in most countries their demands were met around 1920. At this time in many European countries the political or electoral system was changed to allow the enfranchisement of women. In three countries, Belgium, Greece and Italy, women's suffrage was established immediately after the Second World War, in Portugal this happened when democracy was re-established in 1974.

1.1.1. National governments

All 15 EU countries elect their representatives of the lower chamber directly. The electoral systems of course differ, but the powers of this chamber are quite similar in each country: they concern legislation and control over the government. The three Scandinavian countries have the highest number of women in their parliaments at 33-40%, followed by the Netherlands, Germany and Austria. Three countries have less than 10% women MPs: Greece, France and the United Kingdom.

Nine countries also have an upper chamber. In some countries the members of the Senate are elected directly, in others indirectly, for example by representatives of the regions or provinces. Sometimes the members are appointed. In most systems the upper chamber is dominated by the lower chamber. We find the highest percentage of women in Austria (25%) and in Belgium (24%). In the Netherlands and Germany, the proportion of women is 23% and 19% respectively.

The average percentage of women in the lower chamber is 18 and in the upper house 10.

Women's participation in political decision-making [2]

Country	Date women won the right to vote	Most recent election to lower chamber	% Women in lower chamber	% Women in upper chamber
Belgium	1948	1995	11	24
Denmark	1915	1994	33	—
Germany	1919	1994	26	19
Greece	1952	1993	6	—
Spain	1931	1993	23	13
France	1944	1993 / 1995	6	6
Ireland	1922	1992	13	13
Italy	1945	1994	14	8
Luxembourg	1918	1994	17	—
Netherlands	1919	1994 / 1995	31	23
Austria	1919	1995	25	25
Portugal	1974	1995	12	—
Finland	1906	1995	34	—
Sweden	1919	1994	40	—
United Kingdom	1928	1992	9	7

1.1.2. National governments and heads of State

One of the highest levels of political leadership is a position in the national government. The average proportion of women cabinet ministers in the 15 Member States is 16%; of the 537 members of government there are 84 women. There are four frontrunners: Sweden with a balanced government of 50% men and 50% women; and Finland, Denmark and the Netherlands where more than a third of cabinet members are women. There seems to be a correlation between a low percentage of women MPs and the number of women cabinet members: in Greece, Italy, Portugal and the United Kingdom less than 10% of government members are women. There is no woman prime minister in Europe, but there are four women heads of State: Ireland has an elected woman president and Denmark, the Netherlands and the United Kingdom have a Queen as hereditary head of State.

Women's participation in European cabinets, European Parliament, regions and local councils (percentages) [3]

Country	Date of formation of government	Government	European Parliament	Regional Parliament	Local Council
Belgium	1995	12	32	18	20
Denmark	1994	35	44	31	28
Germany	1994	16	36	29	22
Greece	1995	4	16	#	4
Spain	1994	18	33	19	#
France	1995	13	30	12	21
Ireland	1995	19	27	—	14
Italy	1994	8	13	11	22
Luxembourg	1995	25	33	—	10
Netherlands	1994	35	32	—	22
Austria	1996	29	33	20	#
Portugal	1995	9	8	9 *	11
Finland	1995	39	63	—	30
Sweden	1994	50	45	48	41
United Kingdom	1992	7	18	—	#

#: no data available
—: no regional government
* only the autonomous regions of Azores and Madeira have regional parliaments and governments

1.1.3. European Parliament

Interestingly enough, compared with the national parliaments, we find a far higher representation of women in the European Parliament. In nine of the 15 Member States one third of the Members of the European Parliament are women. Eleven Member States have elected more than 25% women to the European Parliament. The differences are striking for countries such as Greece, France and the United Kingdom, where the representation of women in the European Parliament is double the figure in their national parliaments.

1.1.4. Regional and local level

The representation of women at the regional and local level fluctuates for most countries between 10 and 25%. Exceptions are Sweden, with more than 40% women in the regional and local councils, and Greece with only 4% women councillors. It is suggested that participation of women in local councils is easier to achieve than in national assemblies, because eligibility criteria are less stringent and because, since these are not full-time jobs, council positions are easier to combine with rearing children. This suggestion seems to be true for countries like Belgium and France. In the other Member States more women can be found at a higher level of political decision-making, perhaps because it is easier to use affirmative action policies given the more centralized candidate selection procedures used in these countries.

To conclude, the three Scandinavian Member States clearly lead with regard to the representation of women in political leadership, followed closely by the Netherlands, Germany and Austria. The lowest percentages of women representatives can be find in Greece, the United Kingdom and France and to a lesser extent in Portugal and Italy.

1.2. Arguments underlining the importance of women in political decision-making

Why should there be a balanced participation between women and men in political decision-making? And why is it the task of governments, political parties and women's organizations to ensure this balance? Several arguments in favour of an increase in women's participation in political decision-making are listed below.

1.2.1. Equality between the sexes

The full accomplishment of the universality of human rights requires that equality of the sexes, both *de jure* and *de facto*, is considered a basic human right. Today, equality of rights for all, including the right to full participation in all areas of life, is widely recognized as a basic right in both national and international legal instruments. The Universal Declaration of Human Rights and the Covenant on Economic, Social and Cultural Rights as well as the Covenant on Civic and Political Rights are general texts applicable to everyone. A more specific text is the Convention on the Elimination of all forms of Discrimination against Women. It contains a global programme of action aimed at addressing discriminatory situations that violate basic human rights in all fields of society, it stresses the importance of participation of women in decision-making in general and in politics in particular.

The European Community, and more precisely the European Union has undoubtedly contributed in advancing the notion of equality between women and men. Initially, in 1957 the Treaty establishing the EEC (Article 119) proposed the principle of equal pay for equal work for male and female workers. Starting from this principle, the Council of Ministers adopted directives making equal treatment between women and men a norm for the Member States. Furthermore, the

European Court of Justice established equality as a founding principle of European legislation. Condemnation of direct and indirect discrimination was allowed for. Across the second and especially the third and fourth medium-term Community action programmes on equal opportunities for women and men, the emphasis has been shifted from formal equality to real equality.

1.2.2. Democratic principle

The European Community is founded upon the existence of a representative democracy in each of its Member States. The functioning of a democratic system and the image it projects to its actors, has a determining influence on the whole of society. The ideal of democracy rests on the ideas of progress and social justice. Reflection on the possibilities of how to realize these ideas needs a permanent examination of who can legitimately represent the people and partake in decision-making in the name of everyone. Who talks and who decides? Who determines the law? Who manages daily life in national, regional and local assemblies? Who, by his or her presence, personifies public power? The answer to each of these questions in terms of the categories of men and women — supported by statistics, however incomplete or unsatisfactory — is that it is the males who do this. Men, especially at the highest levels of decision-making, hold a quasi-monopoly in politics. Consequently public office, institutional organizations (juridical or consultative) and democratically elected representation give a masculine image to the role of 'representative of the people'.

A clear under-representation of women in political decision-making poses the problem of the legitimacy of existing political structures. When there are hardly any women participating in decision-making, the legitimacy of the outcome of political decision-making may not be the same for both men and women. This may give rise to public mistrust towards the representative system. An ultimate consequence may be that women will refuse to accept laws and policies that have been drafted or adopted without their participation.

This argument, based on the notion of democracy, deals with the recognition of women's rights to full citizenship and with the implication that these rights must be reflected in the effective participation of women, at all levels of political life. There cannot be a true democracy if women are excluded from positions of power.

1.2.3. Differences of interests

Political participation necessitates the articulation and defence of the interests of the group or groups that are represented. The argument presented here is that women are more aware of their own needs and interests and are therefore better able to push for them. Do women, as a group in society, have certain specific interests which distinguish them from other groups, and will these be better articulated and defended by politicians of the same group?

Women as a group have the following in common:

— a historical deprivation of (political) rights;
— a lower participation rate in the labour force, and one which exhibits both horizontal and vertical segregation;
— a feeling of responsibility to reproduce the labour force and bear children which has resulted in a gendered division of domestic labour. Women are the 'carers' in society.

The interests arising from this collective situation of women can be defined as objective women's interests, in the sense that they are an empirical description of the group situation in which women find themselves, and are therefore independent of any subjective evaluation. On the basis of this definition, concrete women's interests can be presented.

The first category concerns matters of political equality: women's rights, equal decision-making, equal pay, equal education, individualization of taxes and social security. The second category concerns matters such as the re-distribution of paid and unpaid labour, time organization, and care facilities. A third group of women's interests follows from the biological differences between men and women. Examples are matters such as health care, the banning of sexual violence, and traffic in women and children (prostitution). The idea is that women will be more aware, for example, of the need to have control over their own bodies, and therefore of the need for access to family planning, of the need for proper provision in the care of children and others who are physically dependent, and of the need for more protection against sexual violence and harassment.

The acknowledgment of objective women's interests leads to the question whether women politicians have articulated and defended these interests more than male politicians. Empirical research of gender differences in political behaviour show clear differences between male and female politicians in role orientations, issue-orientations and in parliamentary behaviour.[4]

1.2.4. Fresh perspective to politics and decision-making

This argument concerns changes in the political system itself, in terms of the content of political decisions and the culture of decision-making. Referring to the previous argument, it can be argued that women politicians, if there are enough of them (critical mass), can change the focus of politics. Due to their experience and interests, women politicians will be more critical of the traditional definition of politics and will enlarge the scope of it. Issues such as child care, sexuality, and family planning, which were once confined to the private sphere, are now seen as political.

Women can also change the structure and culture of politics. Several studies have shown that women develop leadership styles that differ from those of men. For example, in a study of parliamentarians in the Netherlands, it was found that, more often than their male colleagues, female Members of Parliament (MPs) were of the opinion that they were functioning differently in politics from men. They considered themselves to be more practical, more pragmatic, and to have a greater sensitivity to their constituents. There was also a difference in how they defined their job: women MPs showed a preference to reaching compromises and to sustaining contacts with MPs from other parties. Women paid more attention to attending party conferences, meetings at party centres, and sessions of the parliamentary meetings, and also to considering the views of the electorate and to participating in meetings with social groups. Male MPs were more inclined to mention the importance of parliamentary meetings and sustaining contacts with government members.[5]

Women politicians tend to be more democratic and less confrontational, more open to change, and to have a greater ability to work collectively.[6] Women also criticize the decision-making process as being too centralized, too hierarchical, and too technocratic. It is important to examine the assumption that an augmented female presence in high places would alter the outcome of political deliberation. This is an assumption which lies at the heart of the demand for more women in decision-making.

1.2.5. Efficient use of human resources

Efficient use of human resources is vital in order to face the challenges of tomorrow's Europe. Women comprise half the world's pool of potential talent and ability. Each individual, male or female, and each of the genders have differences in experience, insight and knowledge that can lead to a more rounded, informed public policy, while maximizing the human and material resources of the State to the common good.

These days there are no longer many people who hold the opinion that a woman should not become a politician. To the contrary, there are many reasons why a gender-balanced representation in cabinet and parliament is preferable over a male dominated legislation or government. It strengthens the equality principle and the democratic character of the political bodies and it means an efficient use of potential talent and ability. And as long as men and women perform different tasks and therefore have separate political interests, a balance of men and women parliamentarians articulating and defending interests will increase the legitimate power and responsiveness of political decision-making. We can conclude therefore that without the full participation of women in political decision-making, the political process will be less effective than it should be and to the disadvantage of society as a whole.

Chapter 2
Explaining the under-representation of women: relevant factors

Every society and every political system has its own values, rules and procedures which affect positively and negatively the chances for women to become involved in political decision-making. Women constitute half the population and, now that there are no restrictions on suffrage, they also constitute half the electorate. Voting in general elections is one of the easiest acts of participation. Earlier studies on voting behaviour show a gender gap in the turn-out in parliamentary elections. These days women exercise their right to vote in the same numbers as men.

Political participation in a democracy is not restricted to voting, or to participation in parties or representative bodies. Both women and men are involved in community activities, in interest groups or in individual political activities such as canvassing, contacting civil servants or politicians, signing petitions or demonstrating. Research shows that men are somewhat more likely to participate in these activities than women, and especially in the more traditional forms of participation. However, in all EU countries the gender gap is narrowing.

A specific form of participation is to become a member of a party. Party membership is often a necessary condition for gaining access to the representative bodies. In all the Member States, the political parties play a very prominent role in the selection of candidates for elective office. Not many European citizens belong to a political party. Only in countries such as Belgium and Austria where party membership is an economic or social advantage, does a large percentage of the electorate carry a membership card. Generally we find a lower membership rate for women than for men.

Not every party member is a party activist going to party meetings, discussing party matters or chairing a local party branch. At this level there are fewer women participating actively in the party. The top of the pyramid is formed by the candidates standing for election and by those who are fortunate enough to be elected representatives. We have seen in the previous chapter that at the top of this pyramid women are not well represented and in some countries very poorly represented.

2.1. Pathways into legislation

Academic research has played an important role in defining the problem of the under-representation of women in politics. Since the 1970s quite a lot of research has been carried out studying the limited participation of women.[7] Based on the findings of these studies, it is possible to present an overview of the factors which help or hinder women in their attempt to enter high level political positions.[8] This can be seen in the following table.

Processes of incorporation into political decision-making

Eligible citizens	→ ↓	Pool of potential candidates	→ ↓	Pool of candidates	→ ↓	Political elite
	RECRUITMENT		SELECTION		ELECTION	

institutional factors	*institutional factors*	*institutional factors*
— level of development	— electoral system	— voting procedure
— urbanization	— party ideology	— nomination procedure
— gender division of labour	— selection procedures	
— social climate	— integration of women in politics/ parties	*individual factors*
— political climate/level of corporatism		— electoral attractiveness
— gender equality	*individual factors*	
	— degree of organization	
individual factors	— civic experience	
— structural	— support	
— situational		
— psychological		

Definitions of whom is eligible to stand for office are stated in the Constitution. These often refer to citizenship, a minimum age and not being excluded from the right to vote. The next step, described in the table above as recruitment, defines the number of potential candidates. Recruitment is the process by which people get involved in political and party activities, leading eventually to actual candidacy. The process of selection determines which citizens, from the pool of those who are active in politics, are eventually seen as being qualified for a representative position. In countries with a list system the major part of the pathway to power has been completed with the selection as a party candidate well placed on the list. The election provides the final decision as to which candidates will become members of the representative body.

In each step in this process, **recruitment, selection** and **election**, we distinguish individual and institutional factors affecting the electoral chances of women.[9] The first category addresses the extent to which individual characteristics favour the attainment of a representative position. For example, a high level of educational or professional experience, or coming from a 'politicized' family are advantages when pursuing a political career. On the other hand being married and having small children is a disadvantage to women who are striving to achieve a representative position. Institutional factors affecting the achievement of representation by women, relate to the organization of society as well as to the political system itself.

2.2. Recruitment

2.2.1. Institutional factors

The first institutional factors mentioned are the *level of economic development* and the *degree of urbanization* in a country. Possibilities for women are far less in countries with lower living standards and a smaller degree of urbanization. Although no current trend suggests that equality will be fully achieved in countries either with high or low economic development, there is no doubt that changes are easier to obtain in countries with economic growth. The ability to produce benefits for women (change) will serve to narrow the gap between women and men.

The next category refers to the *gender division of labour*. In many countries the society is organized in a way that leaves little scope for women to get involved in public affairs. Examples are the virtual non-existence of nurseries, the impediments placed by the labour market and tax laws and regulations which continue to reinforce traditional role patterns and inhibit women's employment. All of this has a large impact on the individual development of women.

The political participation of women also depends heavily on the more general *social and political climate* of the country concerned. With regard to the social climate, the predominant religion of a country, for example, strongly affects the level of women's political participation. In general one can say that some religious practices encourage and strengthen *de facto* inequality of women in the family and in society. The negative stance of the Church, especially of the Catholic church, on birth control and abortion also has a negative impact on women's political advancement.

Religion has also been an important factor in the development of the traditional sex-role ideology. In many countries there exist strict notions of male and female roles in society. Based on biological differences in reproductive functions, relatively coherent and complex patterns of ideas, practices and cultural experiences for each sex are constructed (a so-called gender ideology). Part of this gender ideology is that men take care of public and the community affairs, while women nurture the family.

Focusing on the *political climate*, certain regimes can be defined as being more democratic than others. Authoritarian regimes and military governments in general restrict or prevent the practice of democracy and do not favour a high level of participation of women in politics. The 15 EU Member States, however, can all be defined as democratic States.

Another aspect is the *level of corporatism* in a country. In some political systems, the state mediates among social interests so as to contain class conflict and to communicate formally with designated interests. Historically, in the system of corporate interaction, gender conflict has been contained as well, with little or no representation for advocates of gender equality. For example, unions are notorious for having a predominantly male leadership, no matter how large the number of women members. A generally low level of representation in the corporate system, leads consequently to low representation of women in politics.

The last category mentioned in the table is *gender equality*. Countries differ in the adoption of constitutional provisions or laws to promote equality between women and men. Economic equality means that women can rely on equal treatment with male colleagues and have the right to own, manage and inherit property. Social equality refers to the right to enter freely into marriage, equal rights in divorce and other aspects of family law. Political equality can be found in countries where legal impediments to women's political participation are abolished. In countries where this happened at a very early stage, one can expect that relatively more women are involved in politics.

2.2.2. Individual factors

At the individual level different explanations of women's disadvantaged political position can be distinguished: structural factors, situational factors and psycho-logical factors. Most of these explanations can be traced to the existing gender division of labour.[10]

Structural explanations — that is, explanations based on a group's place in the social structure — emphasize differential access to political resources. Many social scientists see the persistence of women's lack of political power as a predictable outcome of the ways in which advantages are distributed in society.[11] Structural factors refer to educational level, professional experience and level of income. Education is one of the greatest forces for change in women's lives. Education influences a woman's chances for paid employment, her age at marriage, her control over childbearing, her exercise of legal and political rights and ... her ability to achieve political power. A high level of education appears to be a necessary condition for becoming involved in political activities. The fact that in many countries women's educational level is lower than men's, diminishes her chances of entering the 'pool of the potential candidates'.

Another important political resource is occupational status. Research has shown that women's participation in political life depends largely on their access to employment, which gives them not only material independence, but also certain professional skills. However, women often occupy an unfavourable situation on the labour market. First, there are still many women who do not perform any paid labour and second, when they do, they often focus their education and career development on the so-called 'nurturing professions'. Besides the fact that these experiences are less valued by those recruiting political leaders, it is also true that women are often concentrated in occupations with little autonomy to decide on their leaves of absence and work hours. Very often women lack the advantages of 'professional convergence'. The third political resource, the level of income, is mainly relevant in political systems where one needs a certain amount of money, for example to campaign. In most European systems however, where one runs on a 'party-ticket' the parties take care of the political campaigns.

Situational factors refer to the circumstances of the majority of women — their role as homemakers. First, the marital status can be a disadvantage for women seeking to enter high-level political positions. Political employers may hold the opinion that mothers are unfit to perform in a legislative position. At present however, being married is not so much a barrier, but having (young) children is. With some exceptions, the political rights given to women are not matched with societal adjustment to accommodate this public role of women. Due to the absence of a support system consisting of child care facilities, flexible working hours, etc., the combination of being a mother of small children and being a politician is very difficult. Mothers are often not able to control the allotment of their time, and the hours of a politician are often unpredictable. There also exists a psychological barrier of the development of guilt, which is discussed under this heading because it is derived from the fact that women are the main child minders. From interviews with women politicians it becomes clear that many of them have a continuous feeling of failing their families.[12] The anticipation of these feelings of guilt about her absence can influence a potential female candidate, as well as the selectors, in a negative way.

A final example with regard to the family circumstances of most women, is the support from the partner. Women politicians admit to the importance of (psychological) support from their husbands. In most cases the partners of women politicians are themselves active in politics.[13] Such support is not evident, especially when the political position of the woman competes with her husband's job. It seems that being a politician, and traditional views about the division of labour in a marriage, are incompatible.

The third group of individual characteristics of importance in the process of recruitment are the *psychological* effects of sex-role socialization and more specifically political socialization. Political socialization is the process by which political relevant values, feelings, knowledge, personal characteristics and capacities are attained.[14] The distinction between the private and the public domain, the related ideas about the social roles of men and women (sex-role socialization) *and* the definition of politics as belonging to the public domain, all combine to result in a lesser transformation of political values and attitudes for girls and women than for boys and men.[15] As a consequence women lack confidence in their own political capabilities. In general, values and qualities associated with politics and expected of politicians are typified as masculine and therefore confirm the 'unnatural relation' between women and politics. It appears that women who do get involved in politics often come from a stimulating political background, e.g. parents who were also politically active.[16]

20

2.3. Selection

2.3.1. Institutional factors

In a comparative analysis of the political influence of women, the *electoral and political system* should be taken into account. Previous research clearly shows the relation between the electoral system and the number of women selected in the parliament. A system of proportional representation, where each party presents a list with candidates, provides better chances for women to be selected for the parliament than a majority system with single member constituencies, in which only one candidate is selected out of many. Male candidates normally stand a better chance in majority systems, since the selectors doubt the electoral appeal of women candidates. With a list system the balance of the parliamentary party in terms of occupational background, political experience and region, but also in terms of gender, can be taken into account.

The *party ideology* of the parties in power is particularly important. Party ideology affects women's political involvement in a number of ways. Liberal thought espouses equal opportunity in a competitive political market, whilst socialist and communist ideology contain specific commitments to female emancipation. Conservative ideology, on the other hand, glorifies female participation in the family rather than politics. Parties with a mid- to left orientation on the ideological spectrum have a track record of high female representation. In general political parties based on specific religious objectives view women's participation negatively, because they do not encourage women's integration in the party and because they bring religious principles into subjects such as the role of women in the family, abortion and sexuality. However in the 1990s, now that the ideological distinctiveness of parties has decreased all over Europe, these consequences for the political integration of women are not so clear any more. Most parties, left or right, secular or non-secular are favourable towards an increased participation of women in party politics.

The third possible factor is the *selection process*. The likelihood that women will be selected is the result of the interplay of three factors:[17]

— who makes the selection;

— the selection criteria used;

— whether there are any special policies to strengthen the position of women candidates.

Depending on the electoral system, it is either the voters or parties that make the initial selection. In most European countries list systems are used, which means that the political party selects the candidates. Whether the selection of candidates is decided by the party leadership or by the local or regional party branches also has an impact on the chances of women candidates to gain a 'secured place' on the list. In general, a decentralized selection process has tended to be disadvantageous for the selection of women. This appears to be because national party leaders are more concerned about male-female balance than local or regional party branches. A decentralized procedure also induces tougher competition, resulting in fewer chances for women to obtain a secured place. Moreover regional party leaders often put forward their own regional candidates, who are often males. Parties also differ in selection criteria. Candidates with higher educational and occupational status tend to be preferred, but it is also valuable to be well known within the party. A long party career brings the necessary reputation, as well as indicating that the candidate will be a trustworthy party representative. The most common route to obtain a high level decision-making position is through previous political positions. All parties view political experience as the most crucial requirement for a potential candidate. Such selection criteria negatively affect women's chances of being selected, since it is often the case that women become members of a party at a later age and perform fewer activities within the party.

The next question is whether there are specific policies to ensure at least selection of some women. There are several instruments providing for minimum levels of female representation: reserved seats (direct and affirmative action in the shape of constitutional safeguards through the system of reserved seats for certain groups, such as women) and quota setting (in which a specific percentage of the candidates selected have to be women). Both mechanisms will be discussed in the next chapter.

Moreover the political involvement of women in a country is determined by the overall *integration of women in politics*. An important mobilizing factor in the demand for gender equality has been the new women's movement emerging in the late 1960s and early 1970s. This challenged established institutions and ideas, and its main aim was defending and expanding women's rights. Women organized themselves, demanding new sex-equality policies, the legalization of abortion, more child care facilities and the establishment of new state agencies to promote equality between women and men. One way of organizing politically is within the political parties. Many political parties have a special division or organization for women party members. These women's organizations can be very useful for integrating women in the political process. Women's organizations can lower the entry barriers for women by providing a training ground for newcomers. They can also provide post-election support. Women moving into a male-dominated environment need to be part of a wider network of women from which they can draw advice and support. Women's organizations can also be considered as a recruitment pool. Leadership positions in the women's wing of a political party often lead to a representative post in the parliamentary party. In addition, women politicians whose backgrounds include involvement in women's organizations are likely to be more committed both to ensuring that the political system is made accessible to other women, and to promoting women's issues.

2.3.2. Individual factors

Above we mentioned the necessity for political *experience* in obtaining a high-level political post. Other individual characteristics also influence the process of selection, for example the involvement of women in non-political organizations. Women have a long history of participation in community, school and religious organizations, where they develop political skills. Involvement in these organizations often means encouragement to run for office, while parties view the organizational *support* a candidate can rely on from them as an attractive asset.

2.4. Election

2.4.1. Institutional factors

Two institutional factors are considered here, *voting procedures* and *nomination procedures*. Voting procedures may produce a barrier to women wanting to serve in public office. Preferential voting is very common in some political systems. This can be an advantage for women candidates, given the fact that, more and more, women voters are tending to vote for a woman candidate. In other political systems, one can weigh votes for individual candidates or one can vote across party lines. Even when it is impossible to elect women who are positioned at the lower part of the list directly with preferential votes, receiving preferential votes is always a boost for women candidates, regardless of their place on the list, because it strengthens their position in the parliamentary party.

There is evidence that women are more likely to be selected for political positions by appointment, than when the system calls for direct election. For example countries where the members of the upper legislative chamber are appointed have larger proportions of women than the lower, elected chambers. One explanation is again the fact that the authorities who make the appointments are more concerned with a balance among relevant groupings, including women.

2.4.2. Individual factors

Electoral attractiveness is not so relevant in electoral systems where lists of candidates are used. Here the majority of the voters vote for a party, i.e. the first name on list, and not for a candidate. However, perceived ideas about electoral appeal of men and women do play a role in 'first past the post' systems. In the 1970s many more citizens in EU countries had more confidence in the competence of a male politician than in that of a woman: in 1975 38% had more confidence in a man, only 8% had more confidence in a woman politician, while 40% said it made no difference. In the 1980s there were about 60% who answered that gender made no difference.[18] The performance of many women politicians has helped to change attitudes in this regard.

There are many barriers along the path to legislation. Some of the barriers are the same for both men and women, but there are also many barriers that especially hinder women in acquiring political power. Countries differ, for example, in the opportunities for women to get access to education and to the labour market. The barriers for many women start with their (lack of) political socialization, which may result in a lower level of political interest, political efficacy and political knowledge than men have. For most women it is also difficult to combine their role as mother of young children with that of being a politician. Politics itself is also not well adjusted to the working hours of mothers with meetings at six and no replacement arrangements for pregnant parliamentarians. However, in some European countries recent changes in the gender division of political resources have meant that women have caught up with men since the 1970s with regard to their education and occupational status. But the number of women in party offices and representative bodies has not increased at the same speed. This reveals the importance of barriers within the selection, such as the selection procedures of political parties and the selection criteria, on women's chances of gaining representation. Knowledge of the factors that may help or hinder women to enter high-level political positions makes it possible to develop strategies to overcome these barriers. Several policy instruments are discussed in the next chapter.

Conclusions Part I

In **Chapter 1** several arguments were presented about why there should be more women participating in political decision-making. As a conclusion to Part 1 of this guide we present one more reason why it is necessary that governments, parties and (women's) organizations involve themselves with strategies for a gender balance in political decision-making: the current crisis of party politics that concerns all the Member States. Ensuring that women are at the centre of political decision-making can be a way to reaffirm political and democratic credentials.

What do we see in most countries these days? First, that people turn their backs on politics and political parties: turn-out at elections is diminishing drastically and membership of political parties is declining in most countries. Second, it seems that political parties no longer perform as intermediaries between government and citizens. These days mass media inform the public about the ideas and policies of the politicians, and opinion polls inform the politicians about the wishes and demands of the public. Third, party choice is highly unpredictable. Determining factors such as background characteristics (education, income, socioeconomic status, age), party ideology and party identification no longer seem to structure peoples voting behaviour. Consequently there is a high floating vote, and short-term factors such as the personality of candidates and current issues are becoming more important in determining party choice. Fourth, in many countries we see a high party fragmentation: new, small parties emerge, while the traditional parties are losing their traditional support. A high party fragmentation means a higher chance of unstable governments. Fifth, extreme right-wing and extreme left-wing parties are gaining relatively more votes than before, while in many European countries we see a steadily growing constituency for non-democratic parties.

Important explanations for these trends are to be found in developments such as the weakening of family, community, school, neighbourhood and religious ties and the diminishing of ideological orientation of citizens and of political parties.

To some political analysts these developments have resulted in a transformation of representative democracy into a so-called interest democracy. Individual interests are the main motivation for political organization. Citizens can still be mobilized, not in political parties but in interest groups. They turn to local, regional and national governments to pursue their own private interests, not because of a general concern with the community.

These shifts and changes in the relations between governments, parties, interest groups and citizens need to be considered our consideration. Many Member States worry about the growing gap between politics, government and citizens, about the role of parties and about the democratic deficit. Different possible reforms are being discussed in order to revive democratic patterns of decision-making.

The inclusion of many more women in political decision-making should also play a role in the debate on political reform. Now that citizens are showing a certain dissatisfaction with the traditional political parties (membership is down whilst political cynicism and distrust is increasing), the campaign to promote a better representation of half of the population can be viewed as a possibility to reaffirm democratic credentials.[19] Following this line of reasoning there is also the question of legitimacy: the more groups of people directly involved in political decision-making, the more legitimate the outcome will be for these groups. Then there is the concern of parties for the female vote. Research on women's voting patterns, for example in Germany, gave cause for worry: young women and women in their 30s and 40s expressed a deep frustration with the large, traditional parties such as the CDU (Christian Democrats) and the SPD (Social Democrats).

Electoral considerations are important driving forces behind the current activities of parties to appoint more women. The fact that women candidates get relatively more preferential votes than their male colleagues will certainly stimulate this process. There is some evidence that, when a party starts paying attention to its women, it becomes more attractive to women voters. For example after the SPD introduced quotas for women party members, the party gained female members.[20] Another example is the Italian Communist Party, the PCI, which while going through an identity crisis and a sharp decline in membership, started to promote women and women's issues. The increasing support for women's causes can be seen as 'an attempt to capture women's electoral support and membership, which for many years belonged to conservative groups'.[21]

Finally, we mentioned empirical evidence that women politicians are more sensitive to their constituents and seem to be closer to the electorate, spending more time in answering correspondence and in participating in meetings with different groups in society.[22] All of this can be helpful in restoring the relationships between parliament and citizens.

To conclude, engaging more women in political decision-making can help restore some of the belief in politics and democracy: it will increase the democratic character of parliament and the legitimacy of decision-making; it can help parties to regain their importance as an intermediary between government and citizens and having more women politicians can help make politics more acceptable and attractive to citizens.

Now it is time to take action and get more women into political decision-making. The tools with which this can be done are described in the second part of this guide.

Part II — Tools

Chapter 3
How to create a gender balance: policy instruments

So far we have covered the first two steps in our analysis of the problem of the under-representation of women in politics. In Chapter 1 we defined the problem: how many women participate in political decision-making and why is the limited representation of women a public concern? In Chapter 2 we discussed a framework explaining the persistent under-representation of women in political leadership. Now it is time to review the various solutions that have been offered to the problem. In this chapter we focus on several policy instruments for increasing the political participation of women. In the first place these policy instruments are meant to be used by the national governments of the Member States, since they are, in many respects, the primary movers in the process of empowering women. However, given the influential role of the political parties who select the political personnel for cabinet and parliament, some of the strategies are directed at them.

In the previous chapter we discussed a framework for explaining women's under-representation in politics, distinguishing individual and institutional barriers. Drawing together these various types of explanation we can distinguish two *types of strategy* to overcome the limited participation of women in decision-making. The first is based on the individual barriers. These imply that women do not share power on an equal basis with men, because of a lack of political resources, such as education, professional status and income or because of lack of political socialization and hence a limited sense of political confidence. When women catch up with men on an educational level, and when they enter the labour market in greater numbers, the idea is that in the long run a balance in political power will be reached. The implications of this strategy are to improve access to educational and occupational opportunities for women.

The second line of reasoning takes the institutional barriers as a starting point and acknowledges the fact that a redistribution of power is involved. In this analysis the main obstacle for women seeking to enter leadership positions is the selection process for each position. Research has shown that these processes remain biased in ways that promote the continued tenure of groups and individuals, predominantly men, who are already in positions of power. Strategies and policies should therefore be aimed at changing these selection processes and criteria to allow both women and men equal access. Such a strategy is the setting of a quota for women's participation. A specific type of strategy belonging to this category is legislation. By legislative measures governments can demand that parties, for example, nominate a certain percentage women for the parliamentary party.

In Chapter 3 the close interdependency of gender equality in political decision-making and gender equality in the economic, social and cultural fields was shown. Access to education and to the labour market are necessary conditions for reaching a balanced participation between men and women in political decision-making. Despite the importance of these types of policy, we restrict our discussion of the pros and cons of policies to those strategies that are directly related to political participation, especially policies that refer to the political selection process. In the table below some examples of strategies for increasing the participation of women in politics are presented — they are grouped by type of strategy.

Examples of strategies for governments and parties

Government	Political party
Type 1: Strategies referring to individual barriers	**Type 1: Strategies referring to individual barriers**
recruitment: Awareness-raising campaigns by funding women's organizations (poster campaigns, television spots, advertisements, etc.)	*recruitment:* Campaigns to mobilize women into becoming party members
recruitment and selection: Training of women by funding special training institutes, women's organizations or political parties	*selection:* Training including cadre training courses for women
selection: Provision of facilities that relieve elected representatives of family responsibilities (allowances to hire child care; maternity leave for women MPs, etc.)	*selection:* 'Shadow-council members' (women who are still hesitant to be nominated for the council assist the elected members in order to gain experience and confidence)
	Funds for child care support for party cadre
Type 2: Strategies referring to institutional barriers	**Type 2: Strategies referring to institutional barriers**
selection: Data bank with names of potential women candidates for public office	*selection:* Adapting selection criteria, removing existing gender biases
recruitment and selection: Financing of political parties (women's wings)	*selection:* Data base of names, background characteristics and career intentions of women party members
selection: Scrutinizing selection procedures and selection criteria of all political positions	*selection:* Quota setting for both internal party structures and electoral bodies
selection: Quota for appointed political positions	*selection:* Alternating men and women on the list of candidates or submitting all-women lists
selection and election: Legislation (changing electoral laws to prescribe that parties nominate a certain percentage of women)	

There are many different policies and strategies that governments and parties can adapt in order to increase the participation of women in politics. In the next paragraphs we will discuss five policy instruments: research, collecting statistics and monitoring; awareness raising; enlarging the recruitment pool; setting of quota; and legislation.

3.1. Research, statistics and monitoring[23]

what:	collection and dissemination of facts and figures on the participation of women in decision-making
how:	under governmental supervision, executed by a government agency (National Bureau of Statistics)
why:	to monitor and analyse the position of women in decision-making in order to define corresponding policies; to estimate the number of women in the recruitment pool

One of the most important tools in affirmative action policies is the collection and publication of relevant statistics. This is the empirical confirmation of women's under-representation in decision-making. In a majority of Member States, statistics on women in politics at all levels are collected by public bodies. Often this is done within the context of an equal opportunities policy. The statistics can be collected by the competent ministries (the Netherlands, Belgium), by the National Statistical Office (Germany, Sweden, Denmark) or by Government agencies for Equality (Commission for Equality and Women's Rights in Portugal, Institute for the Woman in Spain). When statistics are not collected by governmental agencies, women's organizations often perform this task (France).

The dissemination of the figures is the next step. All these statistics should be published at regular intervals and be widely available, especially to political parties and women's organizations involved in campaigns to increase the political participation of women.

Governments can also initiate and finance research projects on the role of women in politics. These can be many different types of research: in some Member States governments have ordered surveys researching the political participation of women; in other countries the focus has been more on the analysis of obstacles leading to the under-representation of women in politics or on the study of legal obstacles to setting up a quota system for advisory bodies.

- In 1991 the Belgian Minister of Employment financed a survey among women candidates for the parliamentary elections in that year.

- In the Netherlands in 1993 the Ministry of Social Affairs commissioned a survey of 4 500 national interest organizations in order to find out how many women were participating on the boards of these organizations. The follow-up consisted of a survey among 2 000 women board members and 100 in-depth interviews with women board members.

- In Spain the Women's Institute has undertaken various surveys. Since 1986 it has held a data bank of qualified women. In 1988 a survey was conducted among the electorate studying the opinions and attitudes of the population on the participation of women in politics, and in 1992 one was conducted on the significance of the participation of women in politics. In 1991 a survey studying women's interest in politics was carried out.

- The Ministry for Women and Youth in Germany funded and published a study on the reasons why so many young women do not vote in elections. The results were presented to key actors and strategies for changing the situation were discussed. One of the concrete results of this was a programme funding women's NGOs operating on regional and local levels to organize information fairs to make women aware of their rights and to encourage them to become active in politics.

- In Greece in 1990 the General Secretariat for Equality and the National Centre for Social Research initiated a study of the political attitudes of Greek women.

- The Portuguese Commission for Equality and Women's Rights ordered a study in 1994 on the theoretical concepts of the political participation of women, especially on the concept of 'parity democracy' (see paragraph 4.5.).

A final example of a strategy in this category is the development of a database or a women's talent bank with names, background characteristics and career intentions of women. Selectors can use this database when searching for suitable candidates.

- The Irish government set up a women's talent bank in 1974 — it researches and provides to the government and the different ministers the names of suitably qualified women to serve on State boards and commissions.

- The Netherlands government established in 1995 an organization called Toplink. Toplink's task is to develop a database consisting of names of qualified women. This database can be of assistance to government agencies, parties, private companies and interest organizations in their search for qualified women for their boards.

Collecting data on the representation of women in political decision-making is an essential step in the process of increasing the participation of women. Governments, political parties and the general public need to be aware of the numbers: how many women take part in political decision-making. To be able to focus governmental policies aiming to improve the situation, it is also advisable to initiate research into the country-specific barriers for women to enter high level political positions. Monitoring is necessary for evaluating the working of certain policies: a (semi)governmental agency should be responsible for collecting data every two years or so and report the trends periodically to the parliament.

3.2. Awareness raising[24]

what:	campaigns aiming to reach a large (targeted) public in order to focus their attention on the importance of a balanced participation of women and men in decision-making
how:	by organizing campaigns or by financing political parties or women's organizations for organizing such activities
why:	to reach a breakthrough in the stereotyped perception that politicians are men; to make the entry of women in politics more acceptable and supported

Governments can play a very important role in changing people's attitudes toward the integration of women in politics. Government agencies can organize an awareness-raising campaign, for example by using specific allotted television time, by publishing popular leaflets, by placing advertisements in papers or by placing posters in public positions.

- In Portugal, the Commission on Equality and Women's Rights organized several conferences, addressing large audiences and published the proceedings. Themes were: 'Women and power' (in 1985); 'Positive actions in favour of equality' (in 1988) and 'Equality, democracy and human rights' (in 1990).[25] In 1993 the Commission screened TV spots on the participation of women in politics.

- The Department of Employment in the United Kingdom, the Governmental Sub-Committee on Women's Issues launched in 1994 a series of high profile touring road shows to let women know what opportunities exist in their local area to get skills training or to return to work. There was a video to accompany this, encouraging women to take decision-making positions at work and in public life.[26]

- In the spring of 1989 the Belgian Secretary of State for Social Emancipation, Miet Smet, invited elected officials to take part in the 'First assembly of municipal elected officials'. She presented them with a 10-item programme for a municipal policy of emancipation.

- In Germany, the Ministry for Women and Youth has, since 1989, organized each year a conference on equality for men and women. The same ministry publishes a brochure informing women about their rights and motivating them to join women's organizations and political parties. In 1993, this ministry organized a conference 'Demokratie mit Frauen' (Democracy with women).

There the minister presented the results of a national survey on political participation by young women.

- In Italy, the National Commission for Equal Opportunities in 1992 ran a campaign for the general elections, titled: 'Piu Voti alle donne, piu valore alla politica' (More votes for women, more values to politics).

- The Ministry of Internal Affairs of the Netherlands organized a conference in 1993 on the political participation of black and migrant women. They also organized a week in February 1994 to celebrate '75 years of women's suffrage'.

- In Spain, since 1993 the Minister of Social Affairs Ms C. Alberdi supported publicly the importance of parity democracy, which in fact contributed, together with quota systems in some political parties, to the considerable increase in the number of women in the national parliament (from 16% in 1993 to 23% in 1996).

Governments, instead of doing it themselves, can also financially support other organizations conducting public awareness-raising campaigns. In several EU Member States, organizations involved in the promotion of women in political decision-making receive public aid. Often these grants are for women's organizations, which are sometimes totally dependent on grants from the (local/ regional) government and sometimes they have their own financial sources. In the 1980s and 1990s women's organizations become more involved in the issue of encouraging more women into politics. In the introduction of her book 'Gender and Party Politics' Lovenduski states:

'during the 1960s and 1970s many second wave feminists were cynical about political institutions and electoral politics, preferring the political autonomy they found in new social movements. By the early 1980s, however, there had been a reconsideration of the importance of mainstream politics and feminists became active members of political parties'. [27]

Many of these women participate in the internal discussions within political parties about how to get more women represented in the parties. At the same time in some countries there are joint efforts of women's groups who set up campaigns trying to increase the number of women in decision-making. They work together in awareness-raising campaigns; they mobilize voters to vote for women candidates, and they put pressure on political parties to nominate more women.

- In Denmark much work is done by the Danish National Council of Women, consisting of 47 women's organizations. The Council disseminates information and takes part in the debate. It puts continuous pressure on politicians and parties by sending letters and by publishing the results after each election. They also mobilize voters to vote for women.

- The Federal Ministry for Women and Youth funds the administrative costs of the national headquarters of the umbrella organization of women's associations, the German Women's Council.

- In Spain several NGOs, like the 'Forum for feminist politics' and the 'Association for the support of the European women's lobby', organize actions aimed at promoting women in political decision-making, usually before the elections. They request the poltical parties to include women's issues in their programmes.

- In 1990 in the Netherlands the Association '1994: Vrouwen kiezen in de politiek' (1994 (election year) electing women in politics) was founded and subsidized by the Dutch government. It combined the activities of 29 separate women's organizations, including several women's wings of political parties, all directed at activating women politically. The participating organizations devised their own activities to achieve these goals and these activities were coordinated by the Association. Since the start of the campaign in March 1993, many activities were organized ranging from training sessions for women who might be interested in becoming local councillors to seminars explaining the objective of the campaign. The group also published campaign material, for example two booklets, one with suggestions on how to construct a local emancipation policy and one with facts about the political participation of women, and with interviews with women councillors.

- In Portugal, the Commission for Equality and Women's Rights subsidizes initiatives of Women's NGOs belonging to its Advisory Council either individually for specific actions or the Platform of NGOs for common actions aiming at increasing women's presence in political decision-making such as the 'First national conference of locally elected women' organized by the Group on Parity Democracy in 1993.

Other examples of campaigns by women's organizations include:

- In 1994 in France, the organization Demain la Parité was created, grouping organizations with the same objective. They publish a newsletter, on the theme of equality in decision-making and organize many activities. With regard to the election of 1998 they want to collect a million petitions demanding a balanced political participation.

- In Ireland the Women's Political Association, founded in 1971, has been the chief organization supporting the drive for women in parliament. Through educational initiatives, awareness raising and seminars, as well as practical support for women candidates, it has provided a channel for aspiring women politicians, and a platform for their political manifestos to gain public attention.

- In the United Kingdom four non-party women's organizations are active: the Menerva Educational Trust, set up in 1988 and concerned to help women develop their full potential in employment and public life; Women in Political Life, founded in 1986 specifically to promote women into public appointments; the *300* groups, founded in 1980 and focusing on promoting women into elected positions at national and local level, and the Fawcett Society which is much older and grew out of the suffragette movement for the enfranchisement of women. It continues to promote women in political decision-making but also promotes other aspects of equality. Between them these organizations raise public awareness, issue newsletters, lobby public authorities, run public events, supply training and so on.

The easiest way to bring about changes is when the general public support these changes. The most effective way to increase the number of women in political decision-making is to take care that selectors and the electorate are aware of the necessity of a balanced participation of men and women in cabinet and legislation. Awareness-raising campaigns are therefore essential. In a number of EU countries governments use their resources such as television time, advertising space etc. for this aim, or they stimulate (women's) organizations or political parties to set up campaigns by subsidizing them.

3.3. Enlarging the recruitment pool

what:	increasing the political involvement of women and men by education and training
how:	by organizing training courses or financing programmes set up by political parties and for women's organizations
why:	to remove barriers for women to participate in political decision-making; to make an efficient use of human resources by having more women participate in decision-making

Why do people become involved in politics? And why are women less often involved with politics than men? Many studies have been conducted into the effects of socialization processes on the learning of political roles. Especially important is the observation that men and women are socialized in a different way which has consequences for their subsequent positions in society. Family, school and peers help in shaping the personalities of boys and girls and decide upon their future social roles. A clear-cut destiny for the majority of women is still motherhood, meaning in most cases the complete care for children and elderly family members.

3.3.1. Political socialization

In the 1970s the picture was quite clear: societies were divided in a domestic, private sphere which was predominantly women's and a public sphere which was men's. Since the world of politics was part of the public sphere, and therefore belonged to the men's world, this explained much of the lack of interest by women. Young women associated politics with aggressiveness and dominance: attitudes which girls were not taught. An American political scientist put it thus in 1977:

'Identification for a young boy means association with the wider social political and economical environment; identification for a young girl means association with home and family and a relationship with the wider environment is only marginal. Specific political responses, which evolve later in childhood, fall into the already evolved framework of non-political orientations'. [28]

The near-complete absence of role models, women politicians, did not help either. Research showed, for example, that *young* girls and boys did not differ much in their political interest. However, when girls grew older it was revealed to them that men's judgements did in fact command more attention and respect in the political sphere and this created, according to the researcher, a 'creeping disillusionment' among girls. [29]

Fortunately in the 1990s this situation has changed in most Member States. Women political leaders are not a rarity anymore. At the highest levels, women such as Mary Robinson in Ireland, Gro Harlun Brundland in Norway, Finnboga-dottir in Iceland, Margaret Thatcher in the United Kingdom mounted the platform and many others followed them as cabinet ministers and MPs. The presence of women political leaders and politicians definitely helps in creating feelings that politics is also a 'woman's job'. This, and the fact that women increased their activities in the labour market and, particularly in the Northern countries, caught up with men in education, have meant that the division between public and private spheres is not so clear cut. As a consequence gender differences in voting and other forms of political participation and political interest are gradually decreasing.

This does not mean of course that socialization into gender roles is no longer a relevant factor. As we discussed in Chapter 3, the fact that many women are socialized to become mothers and housewives has led to a clear under-representation of women in those occupations from which political officials are drawn. The under-representation of women in the eligible pool (lawyers and high-level civil servants for example) still explains to a large extent the absence of women in cabinet and parliament. There are of course two ways to solve this problem: increase the number of women in senior professional positions or change the eligibility requirements. In this chapter we will discuss the latter strategy. But first we turn to the whole electorate and discuss the importance of civic education.

3.3.2. Civic education[30]

It is essential for a stable democratic system that people understand democratic principles for decision-making, that they support these principles and that they participate in the system. Knowledge about the functioning of the political system and one's own role in it is therefore also essential. Surprisingly enough in the current debate about the necessity of political reform to bridge the gap between represented and representatives, hardly any attention is paid to civic education. Civic education can create interest and familiarity with political decision-making and should be part of the compulsory curriculum, from the secondary level on. This is not the place to discuss the content of civic education or the ways of teaching. These will differ from country to country and probably even from school to school. However, at the European seminar on 'Strategies for a gender balance in political decision-making' in March 1995 several strategies were discussed for integrating project learning into schools political education curricula. Examples include:

- Danish schools have a subject called 'Open debate', starting at primary level. During these lessons, current political issues from children's daily lives, such as the establishment of an asylum for refugees or the strikes of civil servants are presented and discussed, thus raising awareness of the issues and strengthening the capacity for free speech from a very early age.

- In Spain, according the General Education Law adopted in 1990, all areas of education should include in a transversal way the study of equal opportunities between women and men in private and public life.

There are schools that link the system of pupil representation to political education. Learning about electoral systems and the rules of decision-making develop different insight, if at the same time as these lessons, elections of pupil representatives are prepared and experienced. These show the children that solutions for the schools daily problems are part of the decision-making process of the student body, from the colour of the paint to the choice between Saturday lessons or longer lessons on the other days of the week. Participation in decision-making at schools gives experience of political argument, campaigning and living with the results of a decision taken democratically by the majority, while trying to protect the right of minorities.

3.3.3. Vocational training and university education

The transition from school to working life is a crucial phase for all young people, not only in terms of future career perspectives, but also with regard to the development of attitudes towards the society in general. University and college students often have the chance to develop political interests by joining various groups and initiatives on campus and by participation in democratic elections for the representation of the student body. Research into career patterns of legislators shows that they are much more likely to have been involved in student activities or decision-making in other organizations such as sports or church organizations. Young working class people, however, usually do not find the time and opportunities to discover comparable political activities as a valuable part of their lives. Educational leave for young people as practiced in some countries can surely be a strategy. But it is obvious that the educational programmes offered must include political education in a way that is tailored to the real life situation of the target group.

- Co-financing by the European Social Fund has made it possible to create curricula combining vocational training, political education and personal development for the target group. Participants in these programmes, for example in Germany, tend to vote in elections (which they had given up doing previously) and to join organizations, unions, women's groups and parties.

- A good example of a training programme developed for women is the Women's University in Norway, Kvinneuniversitetet. They offer a one year course called 'Thinking and caring — management and the feminist perspective'. This programme prepares women for public office and leadership positions in the business world.

Programmes specifically targeted at the enlargement of the recruitment pool for politics are also to be found in the field of further education and training. These programmes help women to acquire the necessary knowledge and skills for running as candidates in local elections or for competing for leadership positions in cultural life, trade unions and other social organizations.

- The Ministry for Social Affairs in the Netherlands, has sponsored several training programmes for women in general and for migrant women in particular. Components of these training schemes are: knowledge of the political body, especially the legal and financial aspects; personal development, including communication and negotiating skills, presentation techniques, handling of the media; time management in working life, political life and at home; psychological support and progress assessment.

- The Swedish Government set up a committee in 1993 to analyse the reasons for the low number of women in top positions in private management and to propose measures which would promote changes in this respect. On the basis of the committee's final report, the Government decided in 1994 to set up a so-called 'private management academy' with the task of furthering knowledge, public debate and active work to increase the number of women in leading positions in private management.

3.3.4. Cadre training

Most large political parties offer training programmes for their members and their cadres, sometimes financed by the government. These are specially directed to train women and men to stand for parliament and deal with campaigning skills, presentation and negotiation techniques and media training.

- The Christian Democratic Party of the Netherlands has set a quota for women to enter the cadre training programme: each year at least 40% of the places have to be taken by women.

- Parties in different Member States offer political internships for young women who can witness the work of experienced women politicians. The experience to date has been that both partners feel very positive about this project: the beginners get a clear understanding of what it means to be a female politician and acquire a lot of practical know-how. The politicians find the intensive contact with young women to be a learning programme for themselves, supplying them with insights on one of their target groups, women voters.

- A similar example is the practice of 'shadow councillor' which is used is several parties in Europe. The idea is that women who are still hesitant to be nominated for the local council, assist the elected council members in order to gain experience and confidence.

An important training ground for parliamentary office or cabinet posts is local politics. Serving in a local council is the entrance path for many women politicians. Eligibility requirements such as level of education, professional status or length of party membership are less stringent for local political office than for national representative bodies, which makes local politics more accessible for women.

Essential for the stability of a democratic system is the support of the people for that system: without a certain amount of support and legitimacy every system will in the long run tumble down. An important tool for learning how a democracy works is civic education. Courses in civic education should be part of the compulsory curricula of secondary education. Political socialization and the building of interest in politics and knowledge of politics continues after school. To participate in voluntary organizations, such as youth organizations or environmental interest groups, is often the start of a political career. This is especially true for women who lack the confidence to stand as a candidate for legislative office, specific training offered by parties for example, is very welcome. Governments do play an active part in this, by subsidizing parties to set up these cadre training programmes for women.

3.4. Adapting selection procedures within political parties

what:	scrutinize recruitment and selection criteria for gender biases and introduce affirmative action policies
how:	by defining new eligibility criteria; introducing quota or alternative men/women lists, maximum periods for holding office, etc.
why:	to overcome the present under-representation of women in political decision making; to institutionalize the access of women into political decision-making so that a balanced representation is not dependent on the political will of one specific government or party leadership

3.4.1. Eligibility requirements

The rules governing eligibility and entry to the business, professional and political worlds differ in many ways. If professionals require certificates, degrees and diplomas, the eligibility criteria for prospective politicians are much more diffuse. As a consequence criteria for candidate selection and public appointments set by parties differ widely from country to country and from party to party. In Chapter 3 the importance of a high level of education and membership of certain professions was underscored. In many parties another important asset is party activism and party service. For example, in the Netherlands and Belgium a party member with aspirations should go to the meetings of the local or regional branches, become a delegate to the national party congress and subsequently chair a local or regional branch and be nominated for the national party board. After five to ten years of party activities there is a high probability of being asked to be a parliamentary candidate.

Selection criteria like these affect women's chances of being selected negatively, because there are fewer women party members and, generally speaking, they are less active than men. As they stand, the recruitment and selection procedures parties use are still biased in ways that promote the continued tenure of groups and individuals, predominantly men, who are in positions of power. Incumbents are very difficult to defeat and open seats for high-level political offices are very rare. The characteristics that are most valued in political leaders are those mainly associated with men. Similarly, the standards by which qualifications for public office are evaluated are defined by men's experiences. Increasing the diversity of characteristics that selectors look for in political leaders would help to bring more women into public office.

3.4.2. Quotas[31]

One of the most controversial policy instruments to create a gender balance in political decision-making is the setting of quotas. In general, support for quotas comes from those 'on the outside wanting in', that is, women within parties. They argue that as far as politics is concerned, it has always been much easier for men to be selected, because of the existence of an informal 100% male quota.

Opponents of quotas claim they are discriminatory, promote token women, and undermine the ethos of equality. They make arguments such that 'It is an insult for selection committees to include a token woman on a board, as a candidate at election, or on a public body. Women want to be judged on merit, not because they wear a skirt'. They insist women should 'make it on their own', with election on meritocratic principles such as talent, qualifications and experience. For a substantial number of business and professional women, quotas connote regulation, protectionism and unnecessary intervention.

What are quotas?

Quotas are transitional or temporary measures, whose aim is to overcome the imbalances that exist between men and women. They are often associated with certain forms of control and sometimes include sanctions. In most cases party quotas are self-imposed and not statutory.

Although very difficult to demonstrate empirically since the presence of quotas is never a single factor holding everything else constant, there are indications that quota setting does help to increase the number of women in leadership positions. In those countries which have reached the 'critical mass' of 35% women in parliament and cabinet we find parties with quotas on candidate selection: Norway, Denmark and Sweden. In Norway quotas have been used for over 20 years, and Norwegian women attribute much of their political success to them.

- One of the first parties which introduced quota was the People's Socialist Party of Denmark. The party agreed in 1977 that in all party bodies and electoral assemblies each sex had a right to at least 40% representation. In 1979 64% of representatives for the party in the Parliament were women. In 1984 quotas were used in the candidate selection for the European parliamentary party and in 1988 the party introduced quotas at the local elections. The quotas were abolished in 1990, but the practice continues to rule.[32]

Quota in practice

In this paragraph we focus on quota setting by political parties. Quotas set by governments, for example in electoral laws, will be discussed in the next paragraph.

In 1992 quotas were used by at least 56 political partes in 34 countries, usually in Socialist or Labour parties. Quotas can apply only for internal party structures and/or for candidate selection. According to the Inter Parliamentarian Union quotas are more commonly implemented for internal party rules than for legislative elections.

- A well known example is the two-stage strategy used in the Norwegian parties. Women in the party first pushed for a quota within party structures. Having 30-40% women at the party boards made it much easier to have the party adopt, at a later stage, quotas for elective bodies.[33]

The issue of quotas raises the issue of sanctions. Many quota regulations do not include a sanction when quotas are not met. The only 'sanction' parties sometimes apply, is the publication of the names of local or regional party bodies that have not met the quotas. Central party boards could of course stop funding these bodies, but such measures draw bad publicity and consequently are not very popular.

Even when quota setting is more a symbolic strategy, it can still have some impact. Quotas have an 'eye-opening effect': party officials in charge of the selection of candidates are more aware than before that women are possible representatives. Quota setting in one party also has an effect on the other political parties. They cannot be left behind, so even when these parties are against quotas, they adopt other policies to increase women's participation as well as to increase the parties' attractiveness to women voters.

The choice of a quota percentage (20, 25, 35, 40 or 50%) can be a matter of pragmatism or of principle. Many European political parties choose a percentage equal to the percentage of their female membership. The principle question in deciding on a quota of course concerns the meaning of representation: do delegates represent party members, voters, the electorate or all citizens? Without going into the philosophical discussion of the concept of political representation, the primary view that delegates represent party members only, is hard to defend. In the majority of European countries, party membership is very low. In the Netherlands for example only 3% of the electorate carries a membership card. The problem with using the percentage of women voters as a quota is that the number of votes coming from men and women fluctuates from election to election: in some elections more women vote for a party, in others more men are attracted to that party.

The concept of parity takes the number of women citizens as a guiding principle in which case 50% of all political positions should be filled by women.

- Sometimes different percentages are used for different positions. The German Socialist Party for example, has a quota of 40% for all internal party structures and one of 33.3% for electoral bodies. In 1998 the latter will also become a quota of 40%.

When a party sets a quota too low, there is a danger that the figure will be used as a *maximum* by selectors, instead of a *minimum* percentage.

- In 1977, the Dutch Labour Party adopted a recommendation that 25% of all seats inside and outside the party should be taken by women. In 1985 this was changed into an official quota. Many times, especially at the local level, this percentage has been used as a ceiling: when 25% women on the lists or on the party boards were reached this was used as an argument for not selecting any more women.

Other strategies

Other quota strategies include alternating names of men and women on the list of candidates or an all-women list.

- The Grünen in the Germany city of Hamburg submitted an all-women list in the local election of 1986. To the surprise of many spectators the party won 10% of the vote.

- The British Labour Party agreed in 1993 to introduce all-women short lists in some of their constituencies.

  'Every second a woman'. The Swedish Social Democratic party adopted in 1994 a recommendation that 50% of all political positions should be filled by women. Given the strength of this party, this decision increased considerably the representation of women in politics.

Quota setting can also be combined with other measures likely to contribute towards the extension of opportunities of access for women to positions of political decision-making. Examples are the imposing of a maximum period for holding office, thus ensuring rotation and abandoning the practice of 'cumul des mandats'.

How can governments persuade political parties into taking all these measures? In the Member States the political parties are autonomous and governments are often reluctant to impose their wishes on them. It could be done of course in those countries where parties are funded by the government. Here the government could impose conditions to the party in question, such as a representation of at least 40% of each sex on the list of candidates as a precondition of receiving public money.

- The Netherlands' government found a way around the 'non-interference policy'. It offered financial support to each political party represented in Parliament, under the condition the money had to be used for activities aiming to increase the number of women in the electoral bodies. All parties, with the exception of a small orthodox Calvinist party, accepted the grant and used the money to hire someone for three years with a brief to formulate affirmative action strategies. Two other orthodox parties, who do not subscribe to the governments' policies on gender equality, used the money for training facilities for women.

The overall impression is that quotas have a positive effect on the selection of women candidates: those parties which have set quotas, have more women as their representatives than those parties without quotas. Quotas have an eye-opening effect on the selectors, who will put more effort into their search for potential women candidates. Another positive feature of quotas in political parties is that they are self-imposed and not statutory. Quotas are also temporary measures. They are to be abolished when the representation of women in the legislature is assured. Especially in those European countries where the representation of women is still very low (less than 25%) governments should put pressure on the parties to set quotas. Governments can first persuade the political parties by convincing them of the success of quota setting and then, if the nomination of women still lags behind, by imposing preconditions when the parties receive public money.

It is important that quotas are combined with other programmes to increase the participation of women in the parties, such as training programmes for the female cadre and a human resource database with the names and career intentions of women party members.

3.5. Legislation [34]

what:	legal measures guaranteeing a gender balance in political decision-making
how:	a critical evaluation of existing legislation and introduction of changes or defining new legislation
why:	to achieve a gender balance in political representation and assure that a balanced representation is not dependent on the political will of one specific government or party leadership

Even more controversial than the use of quotas is the use of legislation designed to achieve the equal political rights of women and men. Especially in those countries where there seems to have been no progress with regard to the political representation of women, the call for constitutional and legislative reforms has been made. The demand for legal measures often goes hand in hand with the notion of 'parity democracy': a model of democracy in which 'women are fully integrated on an equal footing with men at all levels and in all areas of workings of a democratic society'. [35] Legislation, requiring for a 50-50 male-female representation in parliament, is the most direct strategy to achieve parity democracy. The concept of 'parity democracy' is however criticized because, according to its opponents, it sees sexual differences as fundamental and seeks its legitimacy in the fact that humankind consists of two sexes, women and men and the belief that this ought to be represented in strict terms of parity at all levels of representation. [36] Contrary to quota setting, which is a temporary measure designed to bring women quickly into politics and in this way overcome the long term under-representation that women have had to suffer, legislation imposing parity democracy is far more fundamental.

- The Belgian Law of 24 November 1994 imposes a minimum percentage of candidates of the same sex. For elections taking place between 1996 and 1999 party lists must have 25% women candidates. After 1999 the percentage must be 33. This proposal was first introduced in 1992. It then included sanctions: linked to the quotas was the right to obtain a national listing number (a number to be used on the ballot as well as in the campaign), the right to state party funding and the right to reduced postal tariffs for campaign mailings. The Belgian Council of State, who advises on constitutional matters, was favourable to the rule to set a maximum limit of two thirds on candidates of the same gender, but against the sanctions. The argument was that the quota rule respected the constitutional goal of equality between the sexes, to the extent that the quotas can be applied to both male and female candidates. The proposal also permits electoral lists that do not respect the quota rule to take part in elections, so in that sense the principle that all Belgians are equal is not jeopardized. However, the Council of State found the application of sanctions unconstitutional, since 'the right of Belgian men and women to be elected must be guaranteed in an equal way'. In the final version of the law the sanctions have disappeared. Instead it was decided that slots on the lists that are legally reserved for a woman candidate cannot be taken up by male candidates and will stay blank. So lists which do not apply the quota rule, will have to cut a quarter up to a third of their candidates. [37]

- In Italy two electoral laws were adopted in 1993. In Law No 81 of 25 March 1993, Article 5.2 and Article 7.1 state that: 'on the lists of candidates, neither of the two sexes may be represented in an amount greater than two thirds'. Law No 27 of 4 August 1993 adopts new norms for the election of the House of Deputies. This law makes the provision that henceforth elections for the House of Deputies will be on a mixed system: 75% of seats will be elected by a first past the post system; 25% of the seats by a list system. For the latter category, Article 4, paragraph 2 states that: 'Male and female candidates will appear alternately' which means in practice a 50-50 split between men and women candidates.

  However, in July 1995 both laws were annulled by the Italian Constitutional Court, referring to the fact that a fundamental right given to all human beings such as that of running for elections, cannot be given differentiated treatment according to sex.

- In France in 1982 the parliament voted in favour of a minimum quota of 25% women on electoral lists for municipal elections. This law was overturned by the Constitutional Council with the argument that the French Constitution opposes any division into categories of voters and candidates.

What are the arguments in favour of introducing legislation? Advocates see this kind of electoral reform as a logical consequence of the constitutional right to gender equality. For example Article 3 of the Italian Constitution says: 'All citizens have equal social dignity and are equal before the law, without distinction of gender, race, language, religion, political opinions or personal and social conditions. It is the responsibility of the Republic to remove economic and social obstacles which limit the liberty and equality of citizens and which are opposed to the full expansion of the human person and to the participation of all workers in the political, economic and social organization of the country'. The law on electoral organization can be interpreted as the measure required by Article 3 of the Constitution to ensure the rebalancing of the starting conditions of men and women in the political world, in order to achieve substantial equality of access to elected positions.

Legislation in order to increase the participation of women in politics can also be viewed as a logical consequence of the ratification by countries of the Convention on the elimination of all forms of discrimination against women (CEDAW). After all, Article 7 of CEDAW states that governments: 'shall take all appropriate measures to eliminate discrimination against women in the political and public life of the country and, in particular, shall ensure women, on equal terms with men, the right to vote (..), to participate in the formulation of government policy (..) and to hold public office and perform all public functions at all levels of government'.

The main argument in favour however, is that, when implemented, it guarantees success: laws have a mandatory effect and impose an obligation to produce results. For example in Italy between 1993 when the law on the municipal and provincial elections came into effect and the summer of 1995 when the law was abolished, the percentage of women councillors more than doubled (from 6 to 13%).

Other countries have been more hesitant to introduce legislation to promote the participation of women in electoral bodies. One argument used against the introduction of legislation is the fact that it is unconstitutional, referring to the non-discrimination laws that exist in most countries. Opponents to legislation also point out that governments should not interfere with the autonomous positions of political parties, an important asset of modern democracies. One can of course say that parties are subject to regulations of public order anyway, especially when they are partly funded by the government, as is the case in Germany.

- An interesting case in this context is the ruling of the Dutch Court on a political party, SGP, a small orthodox Calvinist party in the Netherlands. This party does not allow women to become members of the party. In the summer of 1994 this was brought to Court with reference to the Netherlands constitution as well as to the penal law which forbids people to discriminate on the bases of race, gender, colour, sexuality. The Court's decision was favourable to the party. The argument was that the party is an organization and the right to free organization (autonomy) was seen as a 'higher' right than the issue of non-discrimination.

At present the Belgian law is the only one in EU countries that refers directly to quotas for electoral offices. In other countries we find laws on the number of men and women in *public committees*, such as external advisory boards, where the issue of autonomy does not arise, since it is the government who appoints the members.

- Denmark introduced in 1985 an Equal Status Act on equality of men and women in public committees. This law provides that all bodies whose activities have a political bearing on society must show a balanced membership, and organizations which propose members for appointment must propose for each position at least one male and one female candidate.

- In Finland the 1987 law on equality states that men and women must sit on committees, consultative councils etc. in as equal a way as possible. In 1995, a quota was included, stating that at least 40% of one or the other sex must sit on committees and consultative bodies. The participation of women in these bodies increased from 25% in the 1980s to 48% in 1996.

- In Sweden the government adopted in 1987 a programme entitled 'The sharing of power, influence and responsibilities between men and women in all spheres of society'. It stated that in 1992 the proportion of women in public councils and bodies on public committees should be 30% while in 1995 it should be 40%. The ultimate aim was a 50-50 representation by 1998.

- The Netherlands government announced in 1992 that from then on it was going to appoint only women to existing advisory committees, until a 50-50 balance was reached, while new committees were not going to be installed if there was not an equal representation of men and women.

- The German federal law on equal opportunities of 1994 includes regulations concerning women's representation in consultative bodies at the federal level and stipulates that each federal authority with the right to propose candidates for consultative bodies must nominate two qualified candidates, a woman and a man for each seat. The authority responsible for the distribution of seats must ascertain that there is a balanced participation of men and women throughout the selection process.

Statistics from those countries where these legal measures were taken in the 1980s show that it is a successful strategy. The participation rate of women in consultative bodies in Denmark for example raised from 11% in 1982 to 24% in 1989; in Norway from 24% in 1980 to 35% in 1989. In the 1980s, both countries introduced an Equal Status Act for advisory bodies.

Legislation designed to achieve a gender balance in political representation is the most direct strategy, but also the most controversial. So far, most EU governments have been reluctant to introduce this kind of legislation, referring to it as unconstitutional and against existing non-discriminatory laws. However, when there is no progress at all and parties refuse to take any measures to increase the participation of women in politics, legislation may be the last resort. It can certainly be used as a threat in the negotiations between governments and political parties.

Chapter 4
An integrated gender balance approach: comprehensive policy programmes

The previous chapters have shown many examples of activities undertaken by national governments to increase the participation of women in politics. However, most of these are *ad hoc* activities, dependent on the political will of the present government. According to European Experts Network 'Women in decision making' an important objective of all Member States should be to elaborate a national policy plan (NPP) for a gender balance in political decision-making in the next five years. NPPs should outline how and when a gender balance in politics will be reached. In this chapter we provide a blueprint of an NPP which could be helpful for governments wishing to formulate their own country-specific NPP.

What is an NPP? First, it refers to an initiative of the government. The government in question has to commit itself to the cause of achieving a gender balance in political decision-making. The NPP should begin with a clear statement from the government that the persistent under-representation of women in politics is unacceptable.

Second, the NPP should provide an institutional and structural framework for activities aiming to increase women's political participation. The existence of an NPP in a country should guarantee implementation of this overall policy. In the long run, implementation should not be dependent on the political will of one specific government.

Third, the objective of the NPP should be explicitly stated: 'the government wants to make efforts to increase the number of women in politics'. This objective can be integrated as part of a more general equal opportunities policy guaranteed in the Constitution or in other laws.

Fourth, the NPP should include concrete policies that form a coherent overall framework. For example, when a government decides to set up a database with names of capable women, it should also start a campaign to make selectors aware of the availability of this databank, as well as a campaign to convince selectors that more women in decision-making positions will be an asset to their companies and organizations.

4.1. National policy plan: contents

The NPP should include:

— Background and objective

— Policy framework

— Political positions to which it applies

— Statistics on number of women currently holding positions

— Process of selection for each political position

— Analysis of barriers for women

— Targets

— Measures

4.1.1. Background and objective

The first item refers to the need mentioned above to state the governmental objective and the need to provide arguments why the increase of women in political decision-making is the government's responsibility. The NPP legitimizes policy making and the actual use of the instruments discussed.

4.1.2. Policy framework

This legitimacy can also be grounded in references to other related pieces of legislation or regulations. Austria, Belgium, Germany, Spain, France, Finland, Greece, Ireland, Italy, Luxembourg, Netherlands and Portugal have a Constitution which refers specifically to the general principle of equality of citizens before the law, adding to this the absence of discrimination based on gender, race, religion etc. Then there are the international agreements such as the Convention against the discrimination of women, which includes a paragraph on the political participation of women. All Member States have ratified this agreement thereby committing themselves to improving the participation of women in politics.

4.1.3. Political positions

There are many different political positions to be filled in a country and each position involves different selection procedures and criteria. There are the appointed positions for which the government is very often responsible and therefore able to set targets and use quota to reach these. The same is true in most countries for appointments to consultative bodies. Governments can often influence these appointments directly.

• In 1992 the Dutch government published its intention to increase the number of women mayors and women members of external advisory boards. The percentage of women mayors increased from 8% in 1991 to 15% in 1995; the percentage of women in consultative bodies from 11% in 1991 to 16% in 1995.

Elective offices require different efforts by governments. Given the autonomous position of political parties in most countries, governments can do no more than outline a strategy for convincing parties. The responsible officers in government can have meetings with party officials on a regular basis in which the parties are asked to outline their positive action plans. The government can provide the parties with lists of possible activities to increase the participation of women in their midst. Governments can go further by providing parties with funds for training or, they can threaten to withhold funds when a certain threshold of women representatives is not met. The choice of policies, however, depends strongly on the type of office and the selection procedures. The best approach in the NPP is to distinguish between different political posts and to outline the best operating procedure for each post.

4.1.4. Statistics

In Chapter 3 we described the power of statistics. The NPP should include percentages of women and men participating in decision-making. This too should be done for each political office separately. Preferably the figures should point out the trends: the increase or decrease in the participation of women.

4.1.5. Selection process and analysis of barriers

As mentioned above, people get selected in a different way for each political post. Insight into the formal and informal procedures of selection is essential to define the right strategy to get women selected. Selection procedures and criteria are biased in such a way that they favour incumbents (men) or the politically experienced (men). Governments can assist parties and women's organizations in uncovering these gender biases.

But other barriers can also discourage women from putting themselves forward as candidates. The NPP should include a detailed outline of the selection procedures and the barriers for women for each political post. On the basis of this information, the appropriate policies can be chosen.

4.1.6. Targets

Setting targets is a very useful policy instrument. These should be time-specific. For example: with every election the target could be at least an increase of 5% of women MPs, councillors etc., or it could be that by the year 2000 50% of all mayors should be women. Targets also have the advantage that they can be monitored. When targets are realistic and yet have not been reached, more activities or other more stringent measures may have to be taken.

- Part of the 1988 programme of the Swedish government to increase female participation in decision-making bodies was the establishment of concrete time-specific targets. By 1992, women's representation on public boards and public committees of inquiry was intended to increase to 30%. By 1995 the aim was to increase this to 40%. The final target is that the government authorities, boards as well as official committees of inquiry, should have an equal representation, which should be achieved in 1998.

Targets, together with the obligation to publish the facts and figures on women's political participation, provide parliaments and women's organizations with a concrete basis for criticism when the targets are not met.

4.1.7. Measures

The main part of the NPP, however, should be a long list of coherent and concrete activities that the government is going to undertake in the next, say, five years. The distinction can be made in the NPP between more general and more specific measures. The general measures refer to other fields than politics, such as education and the labour market. In Chapter 2 we pointed out the interdependency of increasing the participation of women in political positions with increasing access for women to education and to the labour market. In those Member States where separate policy plans exist for reaching equality in education and in the labour market, it will not be necessary to include such measures in the NPP. With regard to the more specific measures, the NPP in each country will carry a different list of intentions and plans. In some Member States governments should focus in the beginning on raising the awareness of women and men that politics is not a man's job and that women can perform the job as well as men. 'Can you imagine a world with 81% men and 19% women?'. In countries where there are enough women in the recruitment pool, but where these women lack confidence and political experience, governments should provide training programmes. Especially in those countries where the representation of women in electoral bodies is still less than 25%, governments should convince parties of the necessity of quotas as a temporary measure with a guarantee of success. The choice of policies is not only country-specific, but is also dependent on the political office in question and the numerical representation of women at that moment. A whole range of concrete policies were presented in Chapter 4. Using this list it is now possible for each government to develop its own, country specific, national policy plan for a gender balance in political decision-making.

Preconditions for the success of a national policy plan are a favourable political climate, a budget and administrative support. Besides governments and parties, women's organizations are also important in creating a positive attitude towards the sharing of political power between women and men. A budget is necessary of course, as it is with almost all policy intentions of governments. However, some measures cost more money than others: setting up talks with parties at regular intervals does not require a lot of money, neither does scrutinizing selection criteria for gender biases. Implementing the NPP should not be defeated because of a lack of funds, since political will is the most important ingredient. Administrative support is another key element in developing the NPP and in its implementation. Experiences in Sweden, the Netherlands and Belgium have shown how important it is to have supportive women and men in key positions within the relevant ministries, people who are really committed to the cause and who can use their position to keep the pressure on.

In the previous chapters we have seen that in most EU countries there is a political willingness to increase the participation of women in political decision-making. We presented many concrete examples of activities by governments directed to achieve a gender balance in politics. However, in most countries these are *ad hoc* activities and not part of an overall policy. In this chapter we introduced a blueprint for a national policy plan that each Member State, with a few country-specific adaptations, can use. The national policy plan outlines how and when a gender balance in political decision-making will be achieved. We conclude this chapter with three examples of government programmes that are currently being implemented, as well as an example of a successful European programme to increase the participation of women in political decision-making.

4.2. Policy programme of Belgium [38]

The objective to promote the participation of women in decision-making is specified in the government agreement of 9 March 1992, which makes the provision in Chapter III, that 'the government will continue resolutely to promote a balanced presence and allocation of jobs between men and women in the various domains of social, economic and political life'. Moreover, it specifically requires the government to 'set up initiatives to encourage better participation of women in political decision-making' (Chapter 3).

4.2.1. A global strategy

The Belgian government carries out activities of various types and at numerous levels to promote and maintain the participation of women in political life. The actions taken by the government complement and reinforce each other, and are therefore aimed at giving this policy a solid base.

On the one hand there are awareness campaigns informing the general public and making them and the political world aware that parity participation between women and men in political life is a necessary element of democracy. On the other hand solidarity amongst women must be promoted and women must be consolidated in their political functions, making them more visible. Finally there are structural and legal measures taken to consolidate the changing mentality in social structures and in the political system itself.

4.2.2. Informing and educating public opinion

The Belgian citizen and the political establishment must take note of the fact that a balanced political representation between men and women is an essential component of democracy. In the past years there have been several awareness-raising campaigns initiated by the government. For example in anticipation of the municipal elections of October 1994, the Minister of Equality, Miet Smet, launched an awareness campaign for which the slogan was: 'Supposing we were to change the face of Belgian politics?'.

The slogan was supported by the picture of a male politician with the face of a woman stuck onto it. This campaign started in mid-January 1994, during the period when the electoral lists were being discussed in the parties. It continued over the course of the next few months. With this campaign the government opted for a long-term awareness in order to effect a change in attitude which has, in the long run, a more profound effect on the general public, candidates and parties. It was also an attempt to create a political climate more favourable to women's equality.

4.2.3. Structural measures

In May 1994 a law was adopted by the legislature which makes provision for a legal disposition aimed at promoting the presence of women on the candidates' lists. From then on a list of candidates may only consist of a maximum of two thirds candidates of the same sex. This disposition will be applied to all electoral levels.

Since the implementation of this programme the services responsible have kept up-to-date statistics regarding the political participation of women at all levels, and have publicized and published them at regular intervals.

4.3. Policy programme of the Netherlands[39]

In 1992 the Dutch government decided to take additional measures to raise the percentage of women in politics and public office. In a specific policy programme submitted by the Cabinet and adopted by the parliament 19 specific measures are mentioned. To name a few:

1. Target figures are set for both the relative increase and an increase in actual numbers of women in politics and public office.

2. The figures are published yearly and the results are sent to parliament together with an analysis of the progress made.

3. The government, that is, the Minister of Internal Affairs and the Junior Minister, hold talks with political parties and other bodies to discuss the importance of the issue and the successes and difficulties. The cabinet will point out to the political parties the possibilities of financial aid, for example for affirmative action or for the installment of a human resource database or for the employment of equality officers.

4. Changes in the electoral system will be scrutinized for possible effects on the selection and election of women.

5. The government will continue to provide grants to various organizations, both women's and other organizations. In 1993 and 1994, for example, the mobilization project 'Women voting in politics', was financed, as well as the European campaign, 'Vote for balance in politics' for the European election.

6. The possibility of replacement (for example during pregnancy) of members of the elected bodies will be investigated.

7. In the career planning of mayors the Ministry of Internal Affairs will pay attention to the exit of (male) mayors to other positions than that of mayor, in order to make place for new candidates, women.

8. The organization of local councils will be invited to discuss its role in informing its members (the local councils) how they can facilitate the combination of council membership and taking care of a family.

9. The demands for the position of becoming a mayor will be made explicitly and sent to the Parliament

10. The provincial commissioners (responsible for the nomination of mayors) will be requested to nominate at least 50% qualified women candidates to the local council committees who make the final selection. Only when there are not enough qualified women candidates can this procedure be set aside. Whenever possible there should be at least one qualified woman on the list of candidates for the mayor position presented to the Minister of Internal Affairs.

11. For those external advisory bodies with less than 15% women members the nominating organizations will be requested only to nominate women candidates. Only when it is proven that no qualified women are available can a male candidate be nominated. For those external advisory boards with more than 15% but less than 50% women members, the nominating organizations will be requested to nominate women.

12. Specific attention should be paid to defining strategies for black and migrant women and increasing their participation as well.

With the acceptance of the programme of action by the parliament, the Ministry of Internal Affairs has set up a project group for the implementation of these measures.

4.4. Policy programme of Sweden [40]

'Sweden today has a government consisting of an equal number of women and men, 11 ministers of each. This balance was deliberately chosen by the Prime Minister in order to create a model for the equality-promoting process in all areas of society.

The government is committed to making equality between women and men a guiding principle of its policy, which was pointed out in the inaugural speech last autumn. The main objective is to review all policy fields from a gender perspective and ensure that all government decisions are in line with this concept. Such an approach can be seen as a cornerstone of good governance and it is coordinated by the Minister for Equality Affairs (who is also Deputy Prime Minister), while all other ministers have the responsibility for the equality perspective in their own fields.' [41]

To make this mainstreaming idea work, the Equality Affairs Division gives support to the ministries and also studies their proposals, bills and other documents of interest from a gender perspective before they are submitted to the Cabinet for a decision. The last general election in Sweden (September 1994) led to a result whereby women now constitute 40% of the members of Parliament and 43% of the standing committees. In the municipalities and county councils, 41 and 48% respectively of the councillors are women. In the election, some political parties — among them the Social Democratic Party — consistently put forward ballots where every second candidate was a woman.

The government of Sweden adopted in 1988 a three-year programme to increase female representation in decision-making bodies in public administration. The programme was approved by Parliament as a part of a wider plan of action for equality, which also set up goals for women and the economy, as well as goals for equal opportunities in the labour market, in education and in the family. This strategy, which is still in force, can be summarized in three steps:

Step 1 — Make the shortage of women visible by presenting actual statistics (to Parliament) every year.

Step 2 — Establish concrete time-specific targets for increasing the proportion of women.

Step 3 — Pursue measures that help to achieve these goals.

The following specific targets were set up:

— By 1992, women's representation on public boards and public committees of inquiry should increase to 30%.

— By 1995, it should increase to 40%.

— The final target is that the government authorities boards as well as the official committees of inquiry should have an equal representation, which was assumed to be possible within a decade, i.e. in 1998.

To achieve these targets the government introduced new internal procedures to ensure better coordination among its own ministries in filling the various government-appointed positions. The Equality Affairs Division, and ultimately the Minister for Equality Affairs, was given the responsibility for supervising, checking and approving in writing each proposed appointment before it is submitted to the Cabinet for a decision.

Since the beginning of the 1980s another procedure was already in use. This implies that the ministries demand the nominating organizations (often political parties and social partners) to come up with two names for every seat, that is, one woman and one man, and then the government makes the final choice in order to get an equal balance.

The government also invited NGOs (political parties, social partners, women's organizations etc.) to carry out projects with the aim of encouraging active efforts to increase female representation. These projects were funded by the state, and more than a hundred projects were launched during the last three years.

The combined effects of these and other activities led to a sharp increase in the female representation both at national and at regional level. An evaluation of this strategy has pointed out that it was just the *combination* of launching projects, introducing procedures within the ministries and making the shortage of women visible which were effective in reaching the goals.

4.5. Activities of the European Commission

4.5.1. Objectives and legislative framework[42]

In the third medium-term Community action programme on equal opportunities for women and men (1991-95), the importance of women in decision-making was for the first time officially recognized. The principle of equal opportunities in the workplace, on which the former programmes had focused, will not be achieved without improving the status of women. Therefore, emphasis was put on the necessity of sufficiently representing women in the media and in the decision-making process.

In 1994, the White Paper on the European social policy also engages the Commission to continue its research, information and training activities concerning an increased participation of women in private and public decision-making, and to undertake actions in this field.

The fourth medium-term Community action programme on equal opportunities for women and men (1996-2000) goes a step further. It explicitly states that promoting a gender balance in decision-making is one of the six main aims of the programme.

In March 1995, the European Council adopted a resolution on the balanced participation of women and men in decision-making. Following this the Commission presented a proposal for a Council recommendation on the balanced participation of women and men in decision-making discussed during the Italian Presidency of the first half of 1996.

4.5.2. Instruments

In order to achieve this aim the European Commission mainly made an appeal to two instruments: the European expert network on 'Women in decision-making' and a joint financing programme of projects aiming at promoting women in the decision-making process.

The European expert network 'Women in decision-making' was set up in 1992 with the task of examining the hurdles that kept women from attaining decision-making positions, to inform and sensitize the general public on this subject and to devise strategies and instruments to achieve a larger participation of women and men in decision-making. The network functioned through one expert in each Member State and a European coordinator based in Brussels.

Three successive joint-financing programmes were launched in 1993 (on the European elections), in 1994 (on the participation of women in regional and local decision-making) and in 1995 (on facilitating networking of women in decision-making posts in each Member State). The projects to be supported were selected according to the subject and the regulations which had been defined by the European Commission.

4.5.3. Research [43]

Research giving a clear picture of the under-representation of women in decision-making has been largely undertaken. Facts and figures on the participation of women in the different levels of decision-making in the legislative and the executive power at national, regional and local level have been collected and published by the European Expert Network 'Women in decision-making'. The participation of women in the four main political groups of the European Parliament, their participation in decision-making in sectors such as the trade unions, the banking sector, justice, education and public health was examined in coordination with specialized research institutes and universities.

4.5.4. Actions

The experts undertook two types of actions: organization of European conferences and promotion of awareness-raising activities.

The first important conference was organized in **Athens** under the title 'Women in power' (November 1992). It had to promote a wide public debate on the promotion of equal opportunities for women and men in decision-making. In the end, the first European summit of women who have gained positions of high political responsibility, was held. On that occasion the Athens Declaration, with the promise of promoting the participation of women in decision-making according to the principles of equality and democracy, was signed. This symbolic gesture launched an irreversible debate on the political under-representation of women. Two other conferences followed in **Brussels** (March 1994) on the European elections and in **Dublin** (March 1995) on strategies to promote women in political decision-making. The conclusions of this conference form the basis of this guide. A final European conference on this field was organized in collaboration with the Italian Commission on Equal Opportunities under the title 'Women for the renewal of politics and society' in May 1996.

An important awareness-raising activity has no doubt been the campaign to promote women in the European Parliament for the 1994 elections. This action had the double objective of, firstly, developing tools to inform and increase the awareness of the general public on the need for a gender balance in politics; Secondly, aiming to promote the active participation of women in European politics. An 'action-kit' was developed to make the concept available to anyone interested. Its slogan was 'Can you imagine a world with 81% Romeos and 19% Juliets?' The joint financing programme of 1993 contributed to this campaign at Member State level through financial support to some activities. The number of women elected rose from 19.5 to 25.6%.

Another awareness-raising tool is the brochure on 'Women in decision-making: facts and figures on women in political and public decision-making in Europe'. It contains basic information on a European scale and is published in all the languages of the European Union.

Concluding remarks

The Member States vary in their concern for the under-representation of women in politics. But, despite the fact that in some EU countries the political representation of women is still very low, in most countries governments acknowledge the problem of women's under-representation in politics and recognize the importance of a gender balance in decision-making offices. What is lacking are concrete policies and strategies to increase women's participation and a willingness to implement these policies. Enough research has been carried out studying women's lack of political power. On the bases of an overview of obstacles for women wanting to participate in political decision-making, it has been possible to formulate specific policies and instruments to increase the number of women in politics. This guide assists governments, political parties and (women's) organizations in deciding on their policies to increase the number of women involved in political decision-making. This is not an impossible task, as the many concrete examples show. The blueprint of a national policy plan shows how to integrate the separate policies into an overall governmental policy. Some European countries are already on the right track with a special programme to increase women's political participation. Others still have to follow and for them this guide can be the point of departure.

It is time for a fresh perspective on political decision-making. We mentioned several arguments why governments, parties and organizations should engage themselves in getting more women into political decision-making. It is an implementation of the equality principle found in many European constitutions, it deepens the democratic character of the political system and it increases the legitimacy as well as the responsiveness of the representative bodies. To this we added another argument: restoration of belief in politics and democracy. Politics and political parties are in crisis, now that, in many European countries, people turn their backs on them, and turn-out at elections is low.

Women have brought a variety of issues into the political arena. The agenda of European legal texts now contain issues such as child care facilities, abortion and reproductive rights and sexual violence. Given the still existing gender differences in society, many women politicians will also bring with them a different attitude towards parliamentary work: they are closer to the electorate and spend more time in answering correspondence and in meeting groups of citizens.

The politics of today *needs* more women in its midst to restore some of the belief in politics and democracy.

Notes

1. Schokking J.C., *De vrouw in de Nederlandse Politiek,* Assen: van Gorkum, 1958: 29, 30.
2. Source: *European Experts Network, Women in decision-making. 'Facts and figures on women in political and public decison-making in Europe',* March 1996.
3. Source: *European Experts Network, Women in decision-making. 'Facts and figures on women in political and public decison-making in Europe',* March 1996.
4. There are many examples of research results showing that men and women politicians behave differently. To give some examples:

   About Finland: 'The most noticeable sex differences are the extent to which women MPs concern themselves with bills related to social legislation, and to cultural and educational policies, whereas men MPs concern themselves with transport, public utilities and economic policy' (S. Sinkkonen and E. Haavio-Mannila, 'The impact of the women's movement and legislative activity of women MPs on social development', in: M. Rendel (ed.) *Women power and political systems,* London, Croom Helm, 1981, p. 204).

   About Sweden: 'The proposals put forward by women converged on problems of education and social policy and very rarely with, say, finance questions. On the other hand, motions put forward by men dealt primarily with fiscal matters, trade and industry' (Hogberg, 1981, p. 21, cited in T. Skard and E. Haavio-Mannila, *Unfinished democracy: Women in the Nordic countries,* Oxford, Pergamon Press, 1985, p. 74).

   About the UK: 'The twenty-five Private Members' Bills which have been successfully introduced by women do seem to show a preference for women's concerns. No less than three relate to alcohol or drunkenness, three to protection of animals, nine to women and children directly and four to consumer interests' (E. Vallance, *Women in the House,* London, Athlone Press: 1979, p. 107).

   About the Netherlands: 'A clear difference in the behaviour of women and men politicians is the division of tasks according to gender, a difference which was already apparent when the first woman entered Parliament. Women have tended to occupy themselves more with social functions customarily attributed to women: welfare, health, education, emancipation and the like. This division of labour between women and men MPs has lost some of its sharpness in the 1970s and the 1980s — some women now feature in foreign and defence committees — but is has by no means disappeared'. (M. Leijenaar, 1989, p. 269).
5. Leijenaar M.H., *De Geschade Heerlijkheid. Mannen en Vrouwen in de Nederlandse Politiek, 1918-88,* SDU uitgeverij, 1989, p. 269.
6. Statham, 1987, pp. 409-429.
7. See for references Nelson B. and Chowdhurry N. (eds) *Women and politics worldwide,* Yale University Press, USA, 1994.
8. I used a similar framework before in my dissertation research *De Geschade Heerjkheid. Mannen en Vrouwen in de Nederlandse Politiek, 1918-88, SDU* uitgeverij, 1989, as well as in *Women in politics and decision-making in the Late Twentieth Century,* Martinus Nijhoff Publishers, 1992.
9. Leijenaar, 1989.
10. Welch S., 'Women as political animals', *American Journal of Political Science,* vol. 21, No 4, 1977, pp. 712-716.
11. Lovenduski J., *Women and European politics, contemporary feminism and public policy,* Harvester Press, London, 1986. p. 129.
12. Mandel R., *In the running, the new woman candidate,* New Haven, Ticknor and Fields, 1981, p. 91.

13. Carroll S., and Strimling W., *Women's routes to elective office,* Rutgers Center for the American woman and politics, 1983, p. 26.
14. Greenstein F., *Children and politics,* Yale: Yale University Press, 1965, p. 4.
15. Kelly R. M. and Boutilier M., *The making of political women.* Chicago, Nelson Hall, 1978, p. 173-183.
16. Leijenaar, 1989, p. 313.
17. See also Leijenaar M.H., 'Politieke vertegenwoordiging van vrouwen', in *Acta Politica,* 1992, p. 222-223.
18. *Femmes et hommes de l'Europe en 1983,* Brussels, 1984, p. 121.
19. Vogel-Polsky E., 'Belgium', *Panorama strategies,* Expert Network Women in Decision-making, Equal Opportunities Unit, European Committee, Brussels, 1993.
20. Seeland S., 'Germany', *Panorama Strategies,* Expert Network Women in Decision-making, Equal Opportunities Unit, European Committee, Brussels, 1993, p. 29.
21. Guadagnini M., 'A 'Partitocrazia' without women: the case of the Italian party system', in: Lovenduski and Norris, *Gender and party politics,* Sage, 1993, p. 178.
22. Leijenaar, 1989, p. 269.
23. This paragraph is partly based on the report of Sabine de Bethune: *Strategies to promote women's participation in political decision-making in the European Union Member States, Panorama.* Brussel 1994.
24. This paragraph is partly based on the contributions to the Dublin Conference on 'Strategies for a gender balance in political decision-making' of the Italian member of the Network, Ms. Maria Grazia Ruggerini and the British member of the Network, Ms. Lily M. Segerman-Peck.
25. M.R. Tavares de Silva, 'Portugal', *Panorama Strategies,* Expert Network Women in decision-making, Equal Opportunities Unit, European Committee, Brussels, 1993.
26. Segerman-Peck L.M., 'United Kingdom', *Panorama Strategies,* Expert Network Women in Decision-making, Equal Opportunities Unit, European Committee, Brussels, 1993.
27. Lovenduski J. 'Introduction' in: J. Lovenduski and P. Norris *Gender and party politics,* Sage, London, 1933, p. 1.
28. Diamond I., *Sex roles in the State House,* London, Croom Helm, 1977, p. 34.
29. Currel M., *Political woman,* London, Croom Helm, 1974, p. 161.
30. Part of this paragraph is based on the contribution of the German member of the Network, Ms Suzanne Seeland to the Dublin Conference.
31. This paragraph is partly based on the contribution of the Irish member of the Network, Ms Frances Gardiner, to the Dublin conference.
32. Jacobsen H., 'Denmark', *Panorama strategies,* Expert Network Women in Decision-making, Equal Opportunities Unit, European Committee, Brussels, 1993.
33. Dahlerup D., 'From a small to a large minority: women in Scandinavian politics' in: *Scandinavian political studies,* 1988, vol. 11, No 4, pp. 275-298.
34. This paragraph is partly based on the contributions of Ms Eliane Vogel-Polsky and Ms Françoise Gaspard, respectively the Belgian and French member of the Network, to the Dublin Conference.
35. Van Ebbenhorst-Tengbergen K., 'Presentation of international programme of action to promote the participation of women in decision-making, CDEG, at the Dublin Conference.
36. Outshoorn J., 'Parity democracy: a critical look at a "new" strategy', *paper* prepared for the Workshop Citizenship and Plurality, ECPR Joint Sessions of Workshops, Leiden, 2-5 april 1993.
37. Vogel-Polsky, 1993.
38. This paragraph is based on the speech of Ms. Anne-Marie Servais, adviser in the Office of Ms. M. Smet, Minister for Employment and Labour and responsible for equal opportunities in Belgium at the Conference in Dublin, March 1995.

39. This paragraph is based on the speech of Ms. Benita Plesch, the Secretary General of the Home Affairs Ministry of the Netherlands at the Conference in Dublin, March 1995.
40. This paragraph is based on the speech of Ms M. Lorentzi, Head of the Equality Unit in the Ministry for Social Affairs in Sweden at the Conference in Dublin, March 1995.
41. M. Lorentzi, see note 40.
42. See appendix II.
43. See appendix III.

Appendices

COUNCIL RECOMMENDATION

of 2 December 1996

on the balanced participation of women and men in the decision-making process

(96/694/EC)

THE COUNCIL OF THE EUROPEAN UNION,

Having regard to the Treaty establishing the European Community, and in particular Article 235 thereof,

Having regard to the proposals from the Commission,

Having regard to the opinion of the European Parliament [1],

Having regard to the opinion of the Economic and Social Committee [2],

(1) Whereas the Council has adopted a series of legislative instruments and a number of political commitments in the field of equal treatment and equal opportunities for men and women [3] [4] [5] [6];

---

[1] OJ No C 166, 10.6.1996, p. 276.

[2] OJ No C 204, 15.7.1996, p. 21.

[3] — Council Directive 75/117/EEC of 10 February 1975 on the approximation of the laws of the Member States relating to the application of the principle of equal pay for men and women (OJ No L 45, 19.2.1975, p. 19).
— Council Directive 76/207/EEC of 9 February 1976 on the implementation of the principle of equal treatment for men and women as regards access to employment, vocational training and promotion, and working conditions (OJ No L 39, 14.2.1976, p. 40).
— Council Directive 79/7/EEC of 19 December 1978 on the progressive implementations of the principle of equal treatment for men and women in matters of social security (OJ No L 6, 10.1.1979, p. 24).
— Council Directive 86/378/EEC of 24 July 1986 on the implementation of the principle of equal treatment for men and women in occupational social security schemes (OJ No L 225, 12.8.1986, p. 40).
— Council Directive 86/613/EEC of 11 December 1986 on the application of the principle of equal treatment between men and women engaged in an activity, including agriculture, in a self-employed capacity, and on the protection of self-employed women during pregnancy and motherhood (OJ No L 359, 19.12.1986, p. 56).
— Council Directive 92/85/EEC of 19 October 1992 on the introduction of measures to encourage improvements in the safety and health at work of pregnant workers who have recently given birth or are breastfeeding (OJ No L 348, 28.11.1992, p. 1).

[4] — Council Decision 95/593/EC of 22 December 1995 on a medium-term Community action programme on equal opportunities for men and women (1996-2000) (OJ No L 335, 30.12.1995, p. 37).

[5] — Council recommendation 84/635/EEC of 13 December 1984 on the promotion of positive action for women (OJ No L 331, 19.12.1984, p. 34).
— Council recommendation 92/241/EEC of 31 March 1992 on child care (OJ No L 123, 8.5.1992, p. 16).

[6] — Council resolution of 12 July 1982 on the promotion of equal opportunities for women (OJ No C 186, 21.7.1982, p. 3).
— Council resolution of 7 June 1984 on action to combat unemployment amongst women (OJ No C 161, 21.6.1984, p. 4).

(2) Whereas the Heads of State and Government, meeting within the European Council in Essen, Cannes and Madrid, stressed that the fight against unemployment and equal opportunities for women and men were paramount tasks of the European Union and its Members States;

(3) Whereas attention was focused on women's access to decision-making in Council Recommendation 84/635/EEC of 13 December 1984 on the promotion of positive action for women([1]), in the second Council Resolution of 24 July 1986 on the promotion of equal opportunities for women([2]), in the Council Resolution of 21 May 1991 on the third medium-term Community action programme on equal opportunities for women and men (1991-1995)([3]), in the Council Resolution of 17 March 1995 on the balanced participation of women and men in decision-making([4]) and in Council Decision 95/593/EC of 22 December 1995 on a medium-term Community action programme on equal opportunities for men and women (1996-2000)([5]);

(4) Whereas the European Parliament in its Resolution of 11 February 1994 on women in decision-making bodies([6]) asked the Commission to 'step up implementations of the equal opportunities policy set out in the third Community action programme, to combat individual obstacles which hinder women from taking part in decision-making' and to define 'measures and actions to promote greater participation of women in the decision-making process';

— Resolution of the Council and the Ministers for Education, meeting within the Council, of 3 June 1985 containing an action programme on equal opportunities for girls and boys in education (OJ No C 166, 5.7.1985, p. 1).

— Second Council resolution of 24 July 1986 on the promotion of equal opportunities for women (OJ No C 203, 12.8.1986, p. 2).

— Council resolution of 16 December 1988 on the reintegration and late integration of women into working life (OJ No C 333, 28.12.1988, p. 1).

— Council resolution of 29 May 1990 on the protection of the dignity of women and men at work (OJ No C 157, 27.6.1990, p. 3).

— Council resolution of 21 May 1991 on the third medium-term Community action programme on equal opportunities for women and men (1991-1995) (OJ No C 142, 31.5.1991, p. 1).

— Council resolution of 22 June 1994 on the promotion of equal opportunities for women and men through action by the European Structural Funds (OJ No C 231, 20.8.1994, p. 1).

— Resolution of the Council and of the Representatives of the Governments of the Member States meeting within the Council, of 6 December 1994 on equal participation by women in an employment-intensive economic growth strategy within the European Union (OJ No C 368, 23.12.1994, p. 3).

— Council resolution of 27 March 1995 on the balanced participation of women and men in decision-making (OJ No C 168 4.7.1995, p. 3).

— Resolution of the Council and of the Representatives of the Governments of the Member States, meeting within the Council, of 5 October 1995 on the image of women and men portrayed in advertising and the media (OJ No C 296, 10.11.1995, p. 15).

([1]) OJ No L 331, 19.12.1984, p. 34.
([2]) OJ No C 203, 12.8.1986, p. 2.
([3]) OJ No C 142, 31.5.1991, p. 1.
([4]) OJ No C 168, 4.7.1995, p. 3.
([5]) OJ No L 335, 30.12.1995, p. 37.
([6]) OJ No C 61, 28.2.1994, p. 248.

(5) Whereas the Declaration and the Platform for Action of the Fourth World Conference on Women (Beijing, 4 to 15 September 1995) stressed to need to ensure that responsibilities, powers and rights are shared equally; whereas the Member States are committed to implementing the Platform for Action;

(6) Whereas participation in the decision-making process depends on representation on decision-making bodies at all levels of political, economic, social and cultural life and requires, in particular, presence in posts of responsibility and decision-taking positions;

(7) Whereas women are still under-represented in decision-making bodies, in the political, economic, social and cultural spheres;

(8) Whereas the under-representation of women in decision-making bodies in partly a result of the delay in women attaining equal civic and civil rights, of obstacles to their gaining economic independence and of difficulties in reconciling their working and family life;

(9) Whereas balanced participation of women and men in the decision-making process is a requirement for democracy;

(10) Whereas the under-representation of women in decision-making posts constitutes a loss for society as a whole and may prevent the interests and needs of the entire population from being catered for in full;

(11) Whereas measures aimed at bringing about a balanced participation of women and men in the decision-making process in all sectors should go together with the integration of the dimension of equality of opportunity for women and men in all policies and actions;

(12) Whereas balanced participation of women and men in the decision-making process is likely to give rise to different ideas, values and behaviour which will result in more justice and equality in the world for both men and women;

(13) Whereas the Member States, the social partners, political parties and organizations, non-governmental organizations and the media play a key role in creating a society where there is a gender balance in the exercise of responsibilities in the political, economic, social and cultural spheres;

(14) Whereas it is appropriate to adopt guidelines to promote balanced participation of women and men in the decision-making process with the aim of bringing about equality of opportunity for women and men and whereas it is appropriate, within the framework of the medium-term Community action programme on equal opportunities for men and women (1996-2000), to make those guidelines more effective through the exchange of information on good practice;

(15) Whereas the provisions of this Recommendation apply solely within the limits of Community competence; whereas equal treatment for male and female workers constitutes one of the objectives of the Community, insofar as the harmonization of living and working conditions while maintaining their improvement are, *inter alia*, to be furthered;

(16) Whereas the Treaty does not confer, for the adoption of this Recommendation, any other powers than those referred to in Article 235,

I. RECOMMENDS THAT THE MEMBER STATES:

1. adopt a comprehensive, integrated strategy designed to promote balanced participation of women and men in the decision-making process and develop or introduce the appropriate measures to achieve this, such as, where necessary, legislative and/or regulatory measures and/or incentives;

2. (a) alert those involved in education and training at all levels, including those responsible for teaching material, to the importance of:

   — a realistic and complete image of the roles and abilities of women and men in society, free of prejudice and discriminatory stereotypes,

   — a more balanced sharing of professional, domestic and social responsibilities between women and men, and

   — balanced participation of women and men in the decision-making process at all levels;

   (b) at all levels of education and training, encourage girls and women to take part and express themselves in education and training activities as actively and fully as boys and men, so as to prepare them for an active role in society, including political, economic, social and cultural life, and in particular in decision-making processes;

   (c) make public opinion aware of the importance of disseminating an image of women and men that neither reinforces nor consolidates discriminatory stereotyping of women's and men's responsibilities;

   (d) without encroaching on their autonomy, encourage and support efforts of associations and organizations in all areas of society to promote women's access to the decision-making process and balanced participation by women and men in decision-making bodies;

   (e) without prejudice to their autonomy, encourage and support the efforts of the social partners to promote balanced participation of women and men in their activities and highlight the social partners' responsibility for promoting and proposing women candidates for nomination to various assignments on public commissions and committees in the Member States and at Community level;

(f) devise, launch and promote public campaigns to alert public opinion to the usefulness and advantages for society as a whole of balanced participation by women and men in decision-making;

3. (a) promote or improve the collection and publication of statistics to provide a clearer picture of how women and men are represented at all levels of the decision-making process in the political, economic, social and cultural spheres;

(b) support, develop and encourage quantitative and qualitative studies on the participation of women and men in the decision-making process, and especially:

— on the legal, social or cultural obstacles impeding access to and partici-pation in the decision-making process for persons of either sex,

— on strategies for overcoming such obstacles, and

— on the utility and advantages for society and for the operation of democracy of a better balance between the sexes in the decision-making process;

(c) promote, support and encourage initiatives creating examples of good practice in the various areas of the decision-making process and develop programmes for the dissemination and exchange of experience with a view to propagating activities;

4. (a) promote balanced participation by women and men at all levels in govern-mental bodies and committees;

(b) raise the awareness of those involved of the importance of taking initiatives to achieve balanced participation of women and men in public positions at all levels, paying particular attention to the promotion of a balanced composition in committees, commissions and working parties at national as well as Community level;

(c) provide for, implement or develop a coherent set of measures encouraging equal opportunities in the public sector and respecting the concept of balanced participation in the decision-making process, and ensure, when recruitment competitions take place, that women and men are, as far as possible, represented equally in the committees responsible for preparing competitions and in the selection boards;

71

(d) encourage the private sector to increase the presence of women at all levels of decision-making, notably by the adoption of, or within the framework of, equality plans and positive action programmes;

II. CALLS ON THE INSTITUTIONS, SUBSIDIARY BODIES AND DECENTRALIZED BODIES OF THE EUROPEAN COMMUNITIES TO:

design a strategy for achieving balanced participation by women and men in the decision-making process in each institution, subsidiary body and decentralized body of the European Communities;

III. CALLS ON THE COMMISSION TO:

1. encourage and organize, within the framework of Council Decision 95/593/EC of 22 December 1995 on a medium-term Community action programme on equal opportunities for men and women (1996-2000), systematic pooling of information and experience between Member States on good practice and the assessment of the impact of measures taken to achieve a better balance between women and men in the decision-making process;

2. to this end, and within that framework, step up its efforts to provide information, alert public opinion, encourage research and promote schemes aimed at achieving balanced participation by women and men in the decision-making process;

3. submit a report to the European Parliament, the Council and the Economic and Social Committee, for the first time three years after adoption of this Recommendation and thereafter annually, on its implementation, on the basis of the information provided by the Member States and the institutions, subsidiary bodies and decentralized bodies of the European Communities.

Done at Brussels, 2 December 1996.

For the Council
The President
E. FITZGERALD

II. Charter of Rome — Women for the Renewal of Politics and Society

We, the undersigned, women ministers of different Member States of the European Union, gathered in Rome on 18 May 1996 at the invitation of the President of the European Community Council and on the occasion of the European Summit 'Women for the renewal of politics and society' have together adopted the following Charter:

1. We note a democratic deficit.

Notwithstanding the evolution of the respective roles of women and men in European society, the general statutory recognition of the equality of rights for women and men, and the equal opportunities policies pursued in the Member States of the European Union, we note that the situation of women is still characterized by inequality in most sectors of society. This inequality can be seen in decision-making bodies and authorities, in politics, economics, social and cultural life, and at the local, regional, national and European level, where women are usually in a minority position.

We welcome the research done by the European Expert Network on Women in decision-making and acknowledge that it greatly contributes to increased visibility in this field and that it thereby constitutes a basis for action.

Substantial progress has been made since the Declaration of Athens, adopted in 1992 on the occasion of the first European summit of women in power. This progress, however, is not yet sufficient. In the field of politics, the average female participation in the Member States amounts to 15% for the national parliaments and 16% for the governments; 28% of the present Members of the European Parliament and 25% of the European Commissioners are women.

In other spheres of civil society where decisions are taken that have an indisputable impact on the lives of citizens, both male and female, female representation at decision-making level can be even lower.

We therefore cannot but face the fact that political life and decision-making in general are still dominated by men. This impairs the quality of decision-making and of democracy.

Democracy will acquire a true and dynamic sense when women and men together define the values they wish to uphold in their political, economic, social and cultural life, and together take the relevant decisions.

2. We call for a renewal of politics and society.

The equal participation of women and men in decision-making is an objective that has priority at European level.

This is necessary to reinvigorate democracy and its mechanisms; a balanced sharing of power and responsibilities between women and men will improve the quality of life of the whole population; the representation of all parts of society is indispensable if the problems of European society are to be addressed. The effective implementation of policies to achieve equal participation and partnership between women and men is a priority.

Women, if present in sufficient numbers, contribute to changing politics and decision-making, in terms of the priorities and content, as well as the practices of decision-making.

A renewal of politics and society will be realized with the joint contribution and balanced participation of women and men. This contribution and participation bridge the gap between citizens and politicians, revitalize democracy, and increase citizen confidence in the institutions of democracy.

The equal participation of women at all decision-making levels in economic, social and cultural structures is likewise necessary to guarantee that the needs of women and men are taken into account in all policies, programmes and actions.

3. We declare our commitment to the need to recognize equality of women and men as a priority of the European Union.

The principal responsibility of the Intergovernmental Conference (IGC), which will revise the European treaties, as laid down in the Maastricht Treaty, is to reinforce European democracy by bringing the concepts and structures of Europe closer to its citizens. Representatives of national governments, the European Parliament and the European Commission have declared this to be a priority.

More than half of European citizens are female.

A democratic European society must therefore be built on the effective and real equality of its citizens of both sexes.

We affirm our commitment to the need of enshrining equality between women and men in the new European Union Treaty. We consider it indispensable to integrate a gender perspective into all policies of the European Union (mainstreaming). This lies at the heart of European citizenship and its conditions of practice.

We call on the institutions and organs of the European Union to adopt, urgently, a strategy for achieving an equal participation of women and men and to set concrete targets to that end.

4. We recognize the necessity of concrete action at all levels to promote the equal participation of women and men in decision-making in all spheres of society.

Where progress has been made, notably in the area of public life (in elected assemblies, in councils and consultative committees, etc.), this has been the result of putting into force incentives and/or legislatory or regulatory measures on the part of governments and political parties.

An integrated and specific strategy is necessary if equal participation is to be achieved in all spheres of society. In this light we welcome the Rome Conference 'Women for the renewal of politics and society'.

We commit ourselves to take action for the urgent empowerment of women and to develop the necessary incentives and/or legislative or regulatory measures.

We call upon all actors concerned, male and female, to support this commitment by translating it into concrete actions to empower women and to achieve an equal participation of women and men in the positions of power, influence and decision in all spheres of society.

The initial signatories of the Charter of Rome on 18 May 1996 were Ministers for:

Helga Konrad, Women's Affairs (A)
Miet Smet, Labour and Employment and Equal Opportunities Policy (B)
Jytte Andersen, Labour (DK)
Claudia Nolte, Family Affairs, Senior Citizens, Women and Youth (D)
Vasso Papandreou, Development (EL)
Corinne Lepage, Environment (F)
Nora Owen, Justice (IRL)
Rosy Bindi, Health (I)
Anna Finocchiaro, Equal Opportunities (I)
Livia Turco, Welfare and Family (I)
Marie J. Jacobs, Promotion of Women, Family Affairs, of Disabled and Injured People (L)
E. Borst-Ellers, Health (NL)
Elisa da Costa Guimares Ferreira, Environment (P)
Terttu Huttu-Juntunen, Equality, Social Affairs and FIN
Margareta Winberg, Labour Market (S)

III. List of references to relevant texts

European Union

Third medium-term Community action programme on equal opportunities for women and men 1991-95 (COM(90) 449)

Fourth medium-term Community action programme on equal opportunities for women and men 1996-2000 (COM(95) 381)

Council Resolution of 21 May 1991 on the third medium-term Community action programme on equal opportunities for women and men (1991-95) (OJ No C 142, 31.5.1991, p. 1)

Council Resolution of 27 March 1995 on the balanced participation of women and men in decision-making (OJ No C 168, 4.7.1995, p. 3)

Council Decision of 22 December 1995 on a medium-term Community action programme on equal opportunities for women and men (1996-2000) (OJ No L 335, 30.12.1995, p. 37)

Commission Proposal for a Council Recommendation on the balanced participation of women and men in decision-making, 1995 (COM(95) 593)

Resolution of the European Parliament of 11.2.94 on women in the decision-making process (A3-0035/94, EP 179.623)

Working document of 21.1.96 of a resolution of the European Parliament on the implementation of equal opportunities for women and men in civil services (EP 214.932)

Council of Europe

(These documents can be obtained at: Council of Europe, Directorate of Human Rights, Equality Section, F-67075 Strasbourg Cedex, fax.+33.388.41.27.93)

Recommendation No 1008 (1985) of the Parliamentary Assembly on the place of women in political life (26.4.1985)

Resolution on political life and the strategies to realize equality in political life and in the decision-making process adopted by the Ministers participating at the European Ministerial Conference on the equality between men and women in Strasbourg, 1986

United Nations

(These documents can be obtained at: United Nations, Division for the Advancement of Women, 2 United Nations Plaza, DC2-12th floor, New York, NY 10017, USA, Fax +1.212.963.34.63)

Convention on the political rights of women, 1952

International covenant on civil and political rights, 1960

Convention on the elimination of all forms of discrimination against women, 1979

Strategies for the advancement of women, Nairobi, 1985

Vienna declaration and programme of action — world conference on human rights, 1993

Action platform and declaration of the United Nations Beijing conference, 1995

IV. List of relevant European publications

(These documents can be obtained at: European Commission, DG V.D.5, 200, rue de la Loi, B-1049 Brussels, Fax +32.2.296.35.62)

Studies/reports

European elections 1994. Report of the joint co-financing projects by the European Commission to promote the participation of women in decision-making. European Expert Network 'Women in decision-making', European Commission, DG V, Equal Opportunities Unit, 1994, Doc. V/6468/95 (EN-FR)

Les femmes dans la prise de décision locale et régionale. Actions cofinancées par la Commission Européenne visant à promouvoir la participation des femmes dans la prise de décision, Réseau d'experts européen 'Les femmes dans la prise de décision', Commission Européenne, DG V, Unité pour l'égalité des chances, 1994-95, Doc. V/1125/96 (FR)

La création de réseaux nationaux. Actions cofinancées par la Commission Européenne visant à promouvoir la participation des femmes dans la prise de décision, Réseau d'experts européen 'Les femmes dans la prise de décision', Commission Européenne, DG V, Unité pour l'égalité des chances, 1995-96, (FR)

European elections 1994 — Women standing as candidates and women elected as Members of the European Parliament. European Expert Network 'Women in decision-making', European Commission, DG V, Equal Opportunities Unit, 1994, Doc. V/2078/94 (EN-FR)

PANORAMA

PANORAMA: Strategies to promote Women's participation in political decision-making. European Expert Network 'Women in decision-making', European Commission, DG V, Equal Opportunities Unit, 1994, Doc. V/5962/95 (EN-FR)

Participation of women in four political groups in the European Parliament. European Expert Network 'Women in decision-making', European Commission, DG V, Equal Opportunities Unit, 1994, Doc. V/5953/95 (EN-FR)

PANORAMA: Participation of women in political decision-making at regional and local level. European Expert Network 'Women in decision-making', European Commission, DG V, Equal Opportunities Unit, 1994, Doc. V/6467/95 (EN-FR)

Brochure

Women in decision-making. Facts and figures on women in political and public decision-making in Europe. European Expert Network 'Women in decision-making',

1994, 2nd edition in EN and FR

1995, 3rd edition in GR, NL and SV

1996 4th edition in EN, DE, DA, ES, FI, IT and PT.

PANORAMA: Activities of the European Expert Network 'Women in decision-making' (1992-96), European Commission, DG V, Equal Opportunities Unit

Reports on conferences

Report on the conference and summit 'Women in power' — Athens 1992. European Expert Network 'Women in decision-making', 1992 (EN)

Report on the seminar 'For a gender balance in the European Parliament' — Brussels 1993. European Expert Network 'Women in decision-making', 1993 (EN)

Report on the European Seminar 'Strategies for a gender balance in political decision-making' — Dublin, 23 and 24 March 1995. European Expert Network 'Women in decision-making', European Commission, DG V, Equal Opportunities Unit, 1995, Doc. V/7139/95 (EN)

European Commission

How to create a gender balance in political decision-making — A guide to implementing policies for increasing the participation of women in political decision-making

Monique Leijenaar

Luxembourg: Office for Official Publications of the European Communities

1997 — 79 pp. — 14.8 x 21 cm

ISBN 92-827-9833-X